W. G. Lyttle was proud to be the owner of the first telephone in Bangor. Photograph courtesy and copyright of A. G. Lyttle.

SONS OF THE SOD

A Tale of County Down

W. G. LYTTLE

BOOKS ULSTER

First published in 1886.

This new edition published in 2015 by Books Ulster. Text taken from the undated Belfast edition published by R. Carswell.

Typographical arrangement, introduction, notes and glossary © Books Ulster.

ISBN 978-1-910375-19-8 (Paperback)

ISBN 978-1-910375-20-4 (Kindle)

All rights reserved. No part of this publication may be reproduced, stored in a retrieval system, or transmitted by any means, electronic, mechanical, photocopying or otherwise, without the prior permission of the publisher.

CONTENTS

	Introduction	v
	The Punch Bowl	xiii
I	Sons of the Sod	1
II	Rustic Courtship	9
III	Widow Hunter	16
IV	Black Ben's Proposal	20
V	An Awkward Fix	26
VI	Corney O'Neill	33
VII	A Friend in Need	38
VIII	A Consultation	42
IX	An Eviction	46
X	Squire Brown's Daughter	50
XI	How the News Spread	54
XII	Corney's Wake	58
XIII	Corney's Funeral	68
XIV	Squire Brown	72
XV	Landlord and Bailiff	75
XVI	Landlord and Tenant	78
XVII	The Prodigal's Return	81
XVIII	The Avenger	86
XIX	Ben's Rescue	92
XX	The Course of True Love	97

XXI	Cutting the Churn	103
XXII	Murder	105
XXIII	Who did it?	109
XXIV	On the Track	115
XXV	The Plot thickens	120
XXVI	Dr. Shaw	123
XXVII	In Consultation	127
XXVIII	A Sreak of Light	131
XXIX	Sammy Tamson	136
XXX	Suspense	147
XXXI	A Surprise in Court	153
XXXII	The Real Criminal	159
XXXIII	Retribution	164
XXXIV	Christmas Eve	169
XXXV	Christmas Day	171
XXXVI	Love's Reward	176
XXXVII	A Double Wedding	183
XXXVIII	Dorrey's Hill	187
XXXIX	Another Punch Ball	192
	Glossary	199

INTRODUCTION

In the late Nineteenth Century just about everybody in North Down and the Ards peninsula would have known of W. G. Lyttle. He was a provincial newspaper owner and journalist, a raconteur, and a successful author of local interest books. But he is now more than a century dead and relatively few people in the area today have any knowledge of who he was and the legacy he left behind. Stories of great events played out on the world stage and of prominent people who participated in them are taught in our schools, novels of universal appeal are studied, yet local history and literature are all but entirely disregarded, and so people like Lyttle and their works often fall quickly into obscurity. The republication of the six books in this series[1] aims to raise his profile again in the hope that it will generate renewed interest in the man and his writing and encourage some among the current and future generations to reconnect with their cultural heritage. The following is not intended as a comprehensive biography or bibliography of the works of W. G. Lyttle, nor an academic analysis of his writing. It is merely a rudimentary outline sketch designed to whet the appetite for further study and research among those with the time, inclination and ability. The existing biographical and bibliographical information generally available is patchy to say the least and quite possibly inaccurate in parts. It was, for instance, commonly believed until relatively recently that the author's middle name was 'Guard' but, on examining Lyttle's will and other legal documents, Kenneth Robinson, a librarian and local historian, discovered that his name was actually Wesley *Greenhill* Lyttle. Robinson surmised that the error propagated from an error in the *Belfast News-Letter* obituary which confused W. G. Lyttle with a prominent Methodist minister of the time, the Rev. Wesley Guard.

What we *can* be sure of is that Lyttle was born in Newtownards on the 15th April, 1844, and died in Bangor[2] on the 1st November 1896. This is inscribed on his monument which stands in the grounds of Bangor Abbey.[3] The engraved lettering, which is now partially effaced by time and weather, goes on to read:

> "A man of rare natural gifts, he raised himself to a high position among the journalists of Ireland. He was a brilliant and graceful writer, a true humourist and an accomplished poet. Robin was a kind friend, a genial companion and a true son of County Down."

'Robin' was the name he assumed when giving his humorous recitals around the country in the guise of a County Down farmer and by which he became affectionately known. It was the publication of these readings that merited his inclusion in David James O'Donoghue's *The Poets of Ireland* (1912):

> **LYTTLE, WESLEY GUARD.**—Robin's Readings, eight volumes, 18 —.
> Born April 15, 1844, at Newtownards, Co. Down, and self-educated. Was known all over Ulster as "Robin," author of a great number of poems and sketches in the dialect of a Downshire farmer, which he used to give as public readings in that character. These entertainments were enormously popular, and the eight volumes of "Robin's Readings" ran through various editions. Lyttle also published some stories, such as "Sons of the Sod," "The Smugglers of Strangford Lough," and "Betsy Gray, a Tale of

INTRODUCTION

'98." He was successively a junior reporter, a school teacher, a lecturer on Dr. Corry's "Irish Diorama," a teacher of short-hand (having been, perhaps, the first to teach it publicly in Belfast), an accountant, a newspaper proprietor, editor, and printer. He started *The North Down and Bangor Gazette*, a strong Liberal and Home Rule paper, in 1880. He died on November 1, 1896.

It should be noted that O'Donoghue has erroneously given Lyttle's middle name as 'Guard', but there are other inaccuracies and areas of confusion too. Lyttle founded *The North Down Herald* in 1880, extending the title to *The North Down Herald and Bangor Gazette* in 1883 when he moved the newspaper to Bangor in that year. The full title of *The Smugglers of Strangford Lough* is *Daft Eddie or the Smugglers of Strangford Lough*,[4] and *Betsy Gray, a Tale of '98* is more accurately *Betsy Gray; or, Hearts of Down: A Tale of Ninety-eight*; and *Sons of the Sod* is subtitled 'A Tale of County Down'. It is generally accepted today that there are only three volumes of *Robin's Readings—The Adventures of Paddy M'Quillan, The Adventures of Robert Gordon* and *Life in Ballycuddy*—but in his Preface to the 1968 *Mourne Observer* edition of *Betsy Gray* Aiken McClelland states that these humorous monologues were issued in eight pamphlets after being previously published in the *North Down Herald*. However, Mark Thompson, a Lyttle enthusiast from Ballyhalbert, recently unearthed some advertisements from the *Belfast News-Letter* which indicate that at least part of the series was first published in *The Newry Telegraph* as early as 1878. From the *News-Letter* issue of January 6th 1879 comes the following:

> *The Newry Telegraph*, published on Tuesday, Thursday and Saturday, is on sale, every morning

of publication, at Miss Henderson's, Castle Place, Belfast. The *Telegraph* of Saturday last contained No. 4 of *Paddy M'Quillan's Trip tae Glesgow*. A few copies of 1, 2, and 3 may also still be had.

It is perfectly possible that Lyttle did print what later formed the basis for *Robin's Readings* in the *North Down Herald* but copies of the newspaper are unavailable to check. The British Library only holds the first five issues. No trace of the eight pamphlets mentioned by Aiken McClelland has as yet been found. The story 'The Newtownards Mileeshy' by 'Robin', which was afterwards included in *The Adventures of Robert Gordon* (Part 2 of *Robin's Readings*), appeared in the *Newtownards Chronicle* in three parts during April 1879 and was advertised as 'from his forthcoming *Humorous Readings*'.[5] The second volume was published in Belfast by Allen and Johnston in 1880. A second edition of *Humorous Readings* by 'Robin' was published in 1886. It appears that Lyttle produced his own 'Author's Edition' in 3 volumes as the National Library of Ireland holds Vol. 3, *Life in Ballycuddy* (1892) in its collections. The excellent *A Guide to Irish Fiction 1650-1900* (2006) by Loeber & Loeber refers to a Belfast edition of *Robin's Readings* published by Joseph Blair in 3 volumes in 1893, copies of which are stated to be held at the University of Kansas. R. Carswell & Son of Queen Street, Belfast, also published *Robin's Readings* in 3 volumes, bound in illustrated paper wrappers, in the early part of the 20th Century, but just to add to the confusion they included *Sons of the Sod* as part of the *Robin's Readings* series. They also seem to have mistakenly put the author's initials as 'W. C.' rather than 'W. G.' on at least two of the covers. In a later hardback edition, generally bound in green or blue cloth cloth, Carswell included *The Adventures of Paddy M'Quillan, The Adventures of Robert Gordon* and *Life*

INTRODUCTION

in Ballycuddy in the one volume, but correctly excluded *Sons of the Sod*.

Some tenacious detective work would be required to properly unravel the publication history of *Robin's Readings*, but there is no doubt that the stories included derived from the texts of Lyttle's recitals and that they were first published in collected form as *Humorous Readings* by 'Robin', although the content varied and the text was revised between editions.

There is a degree of confusion too over the chronology of Lyttle's later publications. Rolf and Magda Loeber in *A Guide to Irish Fiction* have it tentatively as *The Bangor Season. What's to be seen and how to see it* (1885), *Sons of the Sod: A Tale of County Down* (1886), *Betsy Gray; or, Hearts of Down: A Tale of Ninety-eight* (1888) and *Daft Eddie or the Smugglers of Strangford Lough* (c.1890), but, apart from *Sons of the Sod*, they could not locate a first edition of any of them. An abridged edition of *The Bangor Season* was published in Belfast by Appletree Press in 1976. *Sons of the Sod* was republished in Bangor by the author's son in 1911 and again c. 1915 by Carswell in Belfast. In 2005 Books Ulster reproduced it as No. 2 in the 'Ulster-Scots Classics' series. An 'Author's Edition' of *Betsy Gray* was published in 1894 and many subsequent editions were produced after that, including a number by Carswell in the early 20th Century and one by the *Mourne Observer*, with an informative, illustrated appendix, in 1968. Another edition, published by Ullans Press in 2008 (No. 4 in the 'Ulster-Scots Classics' series) included an essay on Lyttle and Betsy Gray by Kenneth Robinson. In that he identified the serialization of the book in the *North Down Herald* as beginning on Saturday 7th November 1885. *Daft Eddie*, which according to Robinson was serialized in the *Herald* in 1889, was re-published in an undated edition by Carswell and then in 1979 by the *Mourne Observer*, again with an illustrated appendix. Kenneth Robinson has noted similarities between Lyttle's *Daft Eddie* and a story *The Merry Hearts of Down; A Tale of Killinchy and the Ards* that appeared in issues of the *Newtownards Independent* under the name of 'Rev. J. B.' in February to May 1872. Lyttle also published *Lyttle's North Down Almanac and Directory* from 1880 to 1894.

W. G. Lyttle's performances and stories were extremely popular in their day, especially, of course, in North Down and the Ards. *Robin's Readings* produced no end of amusement because Lyttle (as Robin) was affectionately mimicking the way the locals spoke and put his fictional characters into all sorts of laughter-provoking situations. Even in his more serious books, like *Sons of the Sod* and *Betsy Gray* there are elements of comedy drawn from the dialect and innocence of the common folk. Rather than taking umbrage at being aped in this way and having fun poked at them, they seemed to delight in the celebrity. They understood that Lyttle's intention was not to be condescending or malicious, but that his representations derived from a deep love for the people and their language. The purpose was not to have a joke at their expense, but rather to be a joke in which all could share.

Another reason for his enormous success was that in *Sons of the Sod*, *Betsy Gray* and *Daft Eddie* Lyttle touched on subjects of great interest to the local population. The places, people and events mentioned in his books were obviously very familiar to the community and it therefore identified with them. Historical accuracy was not a primary concern for the author. He was a showman and a salesman first and foremost and, as the saying goes, he would not let the facts get in the way of a good story. Nevertheless, if nothing else, his books provide a valuable source of social and linguistic history for the area, and we are indebted to him for that.

There is still much work to be done on W. G. Lyttle. In the course of preparing this introductory piece other snippets of

INTRODUCTION

information about the man and his writing came to the fore, but as they lead off on tangents that would require deeper investigation they were considered beyond the scope of this essay. Its purpose, as stated earlier, is only to draw a quick vignette with a view to stimulating further research.

In conclusion, it would be remiss not to thank Kenneth Robinson, Mark Thompson and Dr. Philip Robinson who all kindly contributed to this introduction.

Derek Rowlinson,

Bangor,

January, 2015

Notes

1 *The Adventures of Paddy M'Quillan*, *The Adventures of Robert Gordon*, *Life in Ballycuddy* (*Robin's Readings*), *Sons of the Sod*, *Betsy Gray*, and *Daft Eddie*.

2. Lyttle's house stood at the corner of Clifton Road and the Ballyholme Road. It was demolished by the Department of Environment on Saturday 13 March 1982 to make way for a car park. In January 2015, Mrs. Dorothy Malcolm (*née* Adair), who lived on the Stanley Road in Bangor until 1954, proffered the information that the house faced on to the Ballyholme Road (it was, in fact, No.1 Ballyholme Road) and the gable wall and garden adjoined the Clifton Road. She remembers it as being a tall building, three storeys high, with the house name *Mount Herald* displayed above the front door. In her childhood it was owned by a builder called Savage whose daughter Betty taught at Trinity School on the Brunswick Road. Savage had another daughter, Jean, and a son.

3. This is located immediately to the right as one enters the gates to Bangor Abbey.

4. According to Stephen J. Brown in *A Readers' Guide to Irish Fiction* (1910) it was first published as *The Smugglers of Strangford Lough*, c. 1890, but Loeber in *A Guide to Irish Fiction 1650-1900* was unable to locate a copy to confirm this.

5. See *An Index to the Newtownards Chronicle 1873-1900 and the Newtownards Independent 1871-1873* compiled by Kenneth Robinson and published by the South Eastern Education and Library Board Library and Information Service (1990).

THE PUNCH BALL

God bless the hills, the Irish hills,
    Where harvests ripen in the clouds!
God bless the swarthy hand that tills
    To feed the city's sweltering crowds.
        Keep self-honoured,
        As old Slieve Donard,
Shaken as soon by the far world's frown,
        The tall food-growers,
        Where the big blast lowers
At "Hurra for the men of the County Down!"

God bless the ploughs and those who walk
    Elisha-like behind the team;
Bless rack and coulter, beam and sock;
    For labour's an all-holy theme!
        Bless each furrow,
        That, like an arrow,
Gleams in the wealth of its new-born brown,
        Till green points showing
        Where the new bread's growing,
We "Hurra for the ploughs of the County Down!"

God bless the sickles and the sheaves,
    The brawny reaper's sturdy air!
God bless the light of Autumn eves
    Along the maiden's loosened hair!
        Where, leaves rustling,
        She flies a-bustling,
Under their clouds of the golden brown,
        While some good fellow

SONS OF THE SOD

From his stooks right yellow
Sings "Hurra for the girls of the County Down!"

God bless the girls of County Down
    With many a merry boon and churn!
God bless their woers, stark and brown,
    From Cranfield Point to Crawfordsburn!
        Make wives mothers,
        And men like brothers,
High as the heavens o'er the clod or clown,
        Who the axe can't bury
        With a "Hip-hip-hurry!"
At "Hurra for the homes of the County Down!"

The County Down—the County Down—
    God bless the hills of County Down!
May their every hamlet rise a town
    O'er Iron crag and heather brown!
        Hale and hearty
        May creed and party
Mingling their souls every difference drown,
        Like right good fellows,
        Till the world's heart mellows
At "Hurra for the hills of the County Down!"

—Francis Davis.

SONS OF THE SOD
A Tale of County Down

CHAPTER I

The County Down—the County Down—
God bless the hills of County Down!
—Francis Davis.

THE village of Carrowdore is situate in the County of Down, about two miles from Greyabbey, and quite convenient to the old-fashioned pile of stonework called Carrowdore Castle, the Irish residence of the Crommelin family. Carrowdore is locally known as "The Perfect Village," for the reason, doubtless, that no marked changes have been observed in it for several generations. Not infrequently it is spoken of as "the single-breasted village, where the streets are carpeted."

At the period when my story opens—upwards of thirty years ago—the place looked pretty much the same as to-day. The long, straggling street of houses, quaint, old-fashioned, white-washed and thatch-roofed, appears no older to-day than it did then. It is amongst the inhabitants that we must look for signs of change. The hand of time has been busy there. Children have grown up into sturdy, broad-shouldered, bearded men, and buxom, matronly women; young men of that day have grown old; hair that was of raven blackness has turned winter-white, and stalwart forms have bent under the weight of advancing years.

The customs of the neighbourhood, too, are comparatively unchanged. The dress, manners, and mode of living of the people are all much as they were in the good old days. The wants of the people are few and easily satisfied. A festival called a "churn," held by the farmers at the close of their harvesting; a punch dance—called by courtesy a ball; a congregational soirée; a singing at the local schoolhouse; shooting at "Whites" for cocks and hens at Christmas times—these and like harmless amusements now, as then, help to relieve the monotony of life. As to food, the native soil chiefly supplies it, while the inexpensive clothing is mostly procured now, as it was then, from the not far distant town of Newtownards. A native of Carrowdore was once asked by a traveller if he ate much beef. "Beef!" exclaimed the man, "a while see Sam Barr's cart gaun by, but that's my share o't."

But, quiet and unprogressive as the place is, incidents have occurred in its neighbourhood sufficient to stir up the lethargic dwellers in its precincts, and to mark important epochs in the history of many who still live, and of others whose ashes repose under the green and daisy-covered sod of the ancient and beautiful graveyard at Greyabbey. Carrowdore contains not a few relics of the olden times. Notable amongst these are a car and set of harness, believed to have been with Noah in the Ark, and which were handed down from generation to generation. Ultimately these valuable relics were brought to the hammer; the car fell to Wully Yeaman, locally known as the Mayor of Carrowdore, while the harness was knocked down to a man named Foster, who shines it up occasionally with a slice or two of American bacon, a rub of which, he declares, "makes lether weer for iver." The public-house built by a man named Sanderson, well-nigh half a century ago, still stands at Carrowdore. It is now called "The Tenant Right Arms." On the long winter nights many a story of the good old times is told at the "Tenant Right Arms."

At the time of which I write, there stood at a place called "Dorrey's Hill," about a mile from Carrowdore, a large building used as a barn, and which was frequently granted by its good-natured owner for an evening's fun. A dancing class, which was held here by a man named Fullerton, was largely patronised.

In the month of January, 18—, it became known that a "Punch Ball" was to take place at Dorrey's Hill, and cards of admission were freely bought up. The proceeds, after paying for "refreshments," and incidental expenses, were to be devoted towards the relief of a poor and destitute creature named Corney O'Neill, who lived some miles from the place. Young Johnnie Hunter—a prominent personage of our story—was the originator of the ball, but he was aided in this, as in all his other charitable schemes, by "The Mester," or in other words by William Taylor, the teacher of a school located in a certain portion of the Ards. The two young men, who were about the same age, were inseparable. In shooting, courting, and other expeditions they mostly went in company, and wherever they appeared they were general favourites.

It was the night of the dance, and the fun was at its height. There was a large gathering of the lads and lasses, who came from miles around to enjoy a few hours frolic and fun. From Cardy, Greyabbey, Ballywalter, Millisle, Killaughey, and Donaghadee there came not a few, while Ballyhay sent several of its sturdy natives, and there were at least half a dozen lively spirits from Newtownards. The scene to a stranger must have been a novel one. The sound of the quick, emphatic stamping of the dancers' feet was almost drowned by the ringing peals of laughter, the merry shouting, and the cheery strains of Bully Wright's fiddle. Bully—as he was called—though a very young man then, was considered unequalled as a fiddler, and his services were called into requisition at nearly every dance for miles around. Common tallow candles were thrust into iron sockets, manufactured at the smiddy of Tam M'Connell, the nailer, and driven into the walls. The lights, wavering in the draught from the door and the motions of the air caused by the rush of the dancers, threw an uncertain and romantic glare on everything. The walls were bare, rough and utterly unadorned. Rude planks, supported upon sods and large stones, were ranged round the apartment to receive the exhausted dancers, and to accommodate others waiting for their turn. Not a few, however, preferred to sit upon the bare cold floor.

Conspicuous among the female portion of the company was Betty Finlay, who constantly carried in her pocket a tin box which served as her purse, and the coppers in which kept up an incessant rattling while she danced. Another prominent figure was that of a fine-looking young woman from the Ballyboley Moss, who, with a view probably to add to the grace of her movements, had put away her boots in a corner, having previously painted the feet of her stockings, with ordinary shoe-blacking, in imitation of dancing slippers. And there were other blooming damsels, who are still alive, and who as they read, or hear this story read, will doubtless call to memory the merry doings of that night at Dorrey's Hill.

In the corner of the barn, a door, lifted from its hinges, had been laid upon two upright barrels. Perched on a rude three-legged home-made stool placed upon this improvised platform sat Bully Wright, the musician, his eyes fixed upon the figures of the dancers and his mouth apparently doing its best to imitate their movements. A thrashing board lay on the barn floor, and on this Andy Hamilton—a fine, strapping fellow—and a dashing black-haired girl were dancing an Irish jig with an amount of natural grace and action which might have surprised a city onlooker.

The dance had continued for some time and signs of fatigue were becoming visible. The fiddler, as if drawing inspiration from the flying feet, wielded the bow with lightning dexterity; the spectators laughed, clapped their hands and shouted; while above all could be heard the loud "hooghs" of young Jamey M'Briar. At last Andy Hamilton succumbed, kissing his partner, and led her to a seat, amid the cheers of the party. The fiddler took a deep drain from his bottle, the punch passed round, and at the word "Kiss your partners" a series of smacks were heard which indicated that the order was obeyed promptly and with a will.

A brief lull followed, during which the presence of the schoolmaster, who had quietly slipped in, was discovered. Instantly a shout was raised.

"The Mester for a sang!"

The shout was caught up by every voice, while hands were clapped and feet were stamped. Taylor would have declined, but two or three sturdy young fellows lifting him, as though he had been a child, set him on the barn door beside the fiddler. Finding resistance useless, he laughed good-naturedly, and in a rich, mellow voice sang the following old song:—

> A cunnin' wee crayter was auld Robin Young,
> A sly, pawky body as ere went unhung;
> > Though tied to a wifie
> > The plague o' his lifie
> His tricks were a match for the wifikie's tongue.
>
> A grocer was he in a certain big toun;
> An' he coupt up his caupie night, morning, an' noon;
> > Aye watchin', an' joukin'
> > Whan she wasna lookin'
> He winket an' laughted as the drappie ran doon.
>
> An' aye, when the wee drap wad biz in his pow;
> It set a' his couthie auld heart in a lowe;
> > Sae kind to the bairns
> > Wha ran bits o' erran's,
> An han'fu' o' sweeties he aye wad bestowe.

But the wifie bethought her, sae crafty an' crouse,
An' removed the temptation to sell't ben the house;
    Her pressie she locket,
    The key in her pocket,
While Robin sat watchin' as mum as a mouse.

"Tak' warnin', ye auld drunken carlie," quo' she,
"Ye'll ken afore lang what the drinker maun dree;
    Ae drap to your weazen,
    Although it should gizen,
For fechtin' or fleechin' ye'll ne'er get frae me."

O' Robin was mair than a match for her still,
The whiskey she took but she left him the till;
    He gied the waens siller,
    An' sent them ben till her,
An' never ance wanted a glass or a gill.

An' syne how the body would laugh in his sleeve;
An' drink without speerin' the wifikie's leave;
    It sweetened the drappie,
    An' made him sae happy,
To think he could sae weel the wifie deceive!

  Shouts of applause followed upon the Master's song, and he went outside to escape an encore. But a substitute was found in Dominie Harvey who favoured the audience with a local production, a couplet from which will, doubtless, bring it to the minds of many readers:—

"Oh, the knives they were scarce, so the buns they were tore,
And big Nancy Megimpsey she did them devour."

"Noo, boys at it agen an' dinna let the flair cool!" shouted Sam M'Givern, who made a capital "steward" on occasions like this. "Come, lasses," he continued, going round the barn with a hop-step-and-jump, "hae ye a' got a dance?"

Here a laugh was caused by a young fellow called Muckleboy exclaiming—

"There's a lass hasnae had a birl yet; that chestnut yin wi' the white face."

This remark had reference to the girl's red hair and pale countenance, and served to illustrate the ready wit which abounds amongst the "Sons of the Sod" in County Down.

The fun was now resumed in earnest. Dancing was kept up with unflagging zeal till the small hours of morning, while outside an occasional fight served to impart variety to the proceedings. One of these was a rather serious nature. A man named Wully Yeaman—a celebrated pugilist, and known as "the Mayor of Carrowdore"—took offence at another called M'Kay for dancing with his (Yeaman's) sweetheart. He quietly waited till the dance was over, and then going up to M'Kay and touching him on the shoulder, he said—

"Cum ootside, Sam, A want tae speak tae ye."

M'Kay seemed to understand what was wanted, and the two repaired to an adjoining field where they stripped. About twenty of the others gathered round, but no one interfered. The men faced each other promptly, and as they engaged for a moment in a preliminary spar, Yeaman raised a laugh by indulging in his favourite expression—

"Cum on, boy, till a smash ye! A can fecht onything frae a ton wecht tae the wecht o' a blether! Hoogh, Richard, is the crawbar at the daur?"

The fight was a brutal one, and I shall spare my readers a description of it. At the close of an exciting contest Yeaman was covered with blood and bruises, while M'Kay was unable to stand or speak, and presented a frightful aspect. A messenger was dispatched for Johnnie Tennant, the car-driver, and that worthy, having been knocked up out of bed, came upon the scene with his horse and car. M'Kay was placed upon the vehicle and driven, accompanied by two of his friends, John Beck and Davy Askin, to the residence of Dr. Shaw, Greyabbey, who dressed his wounds and administered restoratives.

Other incidents which occurred upon this memorable night are worthy of another chapter.

CHAPTER II

RUSTIC COURTSHIP

IT is not to be understood that the entire time of all the young people who were present in such force at the Carrowdore ball was wholly engrossed by the dancing. There was many a quiet chat in the dark corners of the old building; and out of doors a couple could occasionally be seen walking arm in arm through the adjoining field, enjoying a confidential talk, if not discussing the arrangements for an important change in their mode of life when they should pay a visit to the Rev. David Jeffrey, the Rev. David Parke, or some other local clergyman. Many a sly kiss was that night exchanged in the old barn; many a tryst was made; and, as the small hours of the morning advanced, couple after couple slipped silently away from the crowd of revellers and started upon the homeward journey.

Jeannie Banks and her sister Mary Ann (I shall call them by these names) were undoubtedly the prettiest girls at the dance. I must not define the exact geographical position of their abode; suffice it to say that their father held a fine farm not three miles from Carrowdore, and was one of the most comfortable farmers in the district. He was a large-hearted, hospitable, genial man, proud of his good-looking wife—a Scotchwoman—and of his two handsome daughters. He had enjoyed life himself, when a young fellow and never attempted to prevent his daughters from attending a soiree, concert or dance if they expressed a wish to be present. His wife was of a "canny" disposition, and scrutinised with cautious looks every male visitor who came, as she put it, "tae speir after Jeannie or Mary Ann."

"Hoots, wuman! let the lasses luk efter their sels," Banks would often say to his wife, when she breathed her suspicions regarding certain youths whose fathers were not possessed of broad acres or piles of silver. "Money maks the meer gang, it's true, but it niver made a lad or lass happy yet."

The schoolmaster and young Hunter were frequent visitors at "The Hill"—by which name I shall designate Robert Banks'—and here, as elsewhere, Willie Taylor was a favourite. By Banks and his daughter both were always cordially welcomed; but the mother of the girls received the young men with her accustomed coolness and reserve. So far as Taylor was concerned this did not by any means annoy or disconcert him; he was merely a visitor—not a suitor. With young Hunter it was different. He loved Jeannie deeply and passionately, though he had never been able to summon up sufficient courage to declare his love. Jeannie had guessed his secret, and was far from being displeased. Her mother had guessed it also and more than once had threatened to insist upon a discontinuance of young Hunter's visit to the house.

It was thus that matters stood on the night of the Carrowdore ball, and amongst the first to prepare for home were Jeannie and Mary Ann Banks. The quick eye of Hunter observed their movements, and touching Taylor on the arm he whispered in his ear—

"Jeannie's gaun hame; cum ootside till A speak till ye."

The two young men passed out unobserved.

"Well, Johnnie, and what do you want to say to me?" asked the schoolmaster.

"A'm for seein' Jeannie hame." was the reply.

"It requires no seer to foretell that, Johnnie. Well, Good night, my boy; I must go home alone, I suppose."

"Na, ye'll dae naethin' o' the sort mester; cum alang wi' me, an' them, we'll gang back thegither."

"But why, Johnnie? Sure I would only interfere with you."

Johnnie laughed.

"Yer sharper at yer mathamatiks, mester, nor ye ir at coortin'. Dae ye forget that Mary Ann's wi' her? Shair twa's company, but three's nane!"

"I have you now," said the teacher, and he laughed good-naturedly. "You want me to oblige you by keeping Mary Ann out of earshot. Well, I'll do so with all my heart."

As he spoke, the two girls, muffled up in their shawls, emerged from the barn. They were obliged to pass close by the spot where the young men stood; and as they did so, Hunter caught Mary Ann playfully by the arm.

She started with well assumed fright.

"Bless me heart, Johnnie Hunter!" she exclaimed, "if ye didnae clear scaur the wuts oot o' me."

"Oh, ye hae yer wuts aboot ye still, I think," was Johnnie's answer; and then, in a confidential tone, he whispered, "the mester's gaun till see ye hame," with which brief announcement he left her and the teacher together, and marched off to overtake Jeannie, who had traversed a distance of some twenty yards.

Although Hunter's acquaintance with Jeannie was of some years' standing, he had not yet been able to overcome a shyness of manner when in her company. On the present occasion they walked some distance, side by side, without a single word being exchanged. Jeannie was first to break the silence, and she spoke in the dialect of that portion of County Down, while her accent had something of her mother's broad Scottish twang.

"An' what did ye think o' the dance, Johnnie?" she asked.

"A likit it bravely, Jeannie; agh, wuman, it was the rael guid velye."

"A never heerd better fiddlin' in my life," remarked Jeannie. "Bully is the gran' player, an' nae mistak."

"There's no his aiqual in this pert, A'm shair," chimed in her admirer; "but A'm sayin', Jeannie"—

"What, Johnnie?"

"There was somethin' there that a likit far better nor ether fiddlin' or dancin'."

"An' what was that?" queried Jeannie, demurely, for well she knew what was meant.

"Agh shair ye ken richtly, Jeannie."

"Noo, hoo cud a ken, Johnnie"

Then Hunter's arm stole round her waist, and he whispered in her ear—

"Jest yer ain sweet sel', Jeannie."

The charming girl hung her head, and Johnnie, growing bolder, flung his other arm round her neck and kissed her. Then the girl's indignation seemed to be stirred to its very depth, as, flinging him off, and tossing her head, she exclaimed—

"Johnnie Hunter! dinnae dae that again, my lad. Jest luk hoo ye hae tossed my hair? An' the Mester an' Mary cumin ahint us tae. My guidness! A hope naebody seen ye. Yer a terble imperent fella, so ye ir."

But Jeannie's merry eye belied her sharp tongue, and a minute afterwards she and her sweetheart were trudging along, arm in arm, and engaged in deep and earnest conversation. It would be a breach of confidence to disclose the nature of the lovers' discourse, which was kept up unceasingly until Jeannie's home was reached. Willie Taylor and his companion were standing at the "gable end" awaiting the others.

As Hunter advanced to join their friends he whispered to Jeannie—

"A'm sayin'; shair we may gang in for a while?"

"A doot it's ower late," murmured the girl.

"Blethers, wuman! it's no yin o'clock yet," said Johnnie.

"Weel if a dae let ye in ye maun baith keep gie an' quate."

Then followed a whispered conference between the sisters,

after which they cautiously advanced to the door, Jeannie placing her hand on the latch, and Mary Ann signalling to the young men to follow closely in the rere.

It may not be known to some readers of these pages, who are strangers to the district, that many of the people seldom lock or bar their doors at night. Thieves are almost unknown in the broad Ards, and if an occasional act of burglary does occur it is, as a rule, confined to the appropriation of some fowl, picked up at an out-house. Another custom equally prevails. A lover seeing his sweetheart home is, in most cases, expected to go into the house, however late the hour, and the couple, sitting together beside the remains of the kitchen fire, or in more retired quarters "doon the hoose" (in a room off the kitchen) enjoy each other's society until the fair one deems it judicious that her admirer should take his departure.

As Jeannie raised the latch the growl of a dog was heard. Stepping quickly inside she patted the animal upon the head to allay his disquietude, while Mary Ann and the young fellows glided after her upon tiptoe. Then, from a sleeping loft directly over the kitchen, came in sharp tones the enquiry, in a female voice—

"Is that you, lasses?"

"Yis, ma," answered Jeannie.

"Ye hae ta'en yer times, A'm thinkin'," remarked Mrs. Banks.

"It's no very late, indeed," remonstrated Jeannie.

"Weel, pit the bar in the daur and get till yer beds; ye hae tae churn in the mornin', ye ken."

During the course of this colloquy, Mary Ann had guided the lovers into an adjoining apartment where they were quickly followed by Jeannie; and, forming in couples, they engaged in subdued conversation.

"A'm shair yer hungry, Johnnie," said Jeannie.

"A'm jest stervin'," was the whispered response.

"Whun my ma fa's ower* A'll get ye something tae eat."
Just then the dog emitted a low prolonged growl.
"Dang saze that dug!" muttered Hunter.
"A think A heerd a fut ootside," whispered Jeannie.
"Wha cud it be, A wonner?" queried Hunter.

They listened for a few minutes, but no sound could be heard, and their uneasiness was allayed. Half an hour passed, and Jeannie, in her stocking soles, went in search of food, returning in a brief space of time with bread and butter. A second journey was made, and this time she brought a jug of sweetmilk and a couple of tins.

"Yin maun dae ye baith," she whispered to Mary Ann, handing her a tin, and filling it with milk. Then she joined her companion, who did not object to a drink of rich new milk upon similar conditions. For ten minutes there was a subdued gurgling sound and another of gentle mastication. There was no candle burning, but a full moon, the bright beams of which shone in at the window, supplied sufficient light.

By and by it was time the young men should depart, and Jeannie—who evidently was an experienced hand at the work—slipped off to the kitchen for the purpose of opening the door. She was absent for some time; so long, in fact, that Johnnie, growing impatient, had risen to go in search of her, when she was observed noiselessly entering the room and holding up her hand to enjoin silence. She was breathing heavily and seemed to be considerably agitated.

"What kept ye?" whispered Hunter.
"Oh, Johnnie, what's to be din?" she gasped, "yer tied in!"

Johnnie opened his mouth, evidently to speak his displeasure in no subdued tones; but, quick as lightning, Jeannie placed her hand upon it and stopped his utterance. Then she turned to

---
*Falls asleep (Lyttle's note).

acquaint her sister of the position of affairs, but just at that moment the creaking of footsteps was heard upon the floor overhead. Poor Jeannie sank upon the sofa beside Hunter, and clutching him convulsively by the hand, gasped out in an excited whisper—

"Oh, Johnnie, my ma's cumin' doonstairs!"

CHAPTER III

WIDOW HUNTER

WE must for a brief space leave the youthful lovers in their somewhat awkward predicament, and introduce to our readers other personages who are to figure in our story.

In a northern portion of the broad, pleasant and prosperous Ards there stood a large, unshapely, old-fashioned structure, the residence of a certain country squire, and designated by the people of the country for many miles around "The Big Hoose." The building stood fully a mile from the highway and was approached by an old cart-road, which mangled and torn as it was by the heavily laden carts continually passing over it, sorely tried the springs of the squire's gig. A narrow avenue some three hundred yards in length branched off this cart-road and led to the squire's.

It was a dull, cheerless-looking house, with small windows and narrow entrance. The thatched roof was perforated by hundreds of sparrows, that chattered from the eaves the livelong day, and fattened upon the grain in the adjoining haggard. Trees, aged and sturdy and gnarled, surrounded the house on all sides, adding to its gloomy aspect, and at times effectually excluding what little light the small windows, with their diamond-shaped panes, would have admitted.

Squire Brown, the occupant of this dwelling, was a man advanced in years; a widower, but not childless, who moped and fretted, it was said, over the untimely death of a beautiful wife, upon whom he had lovingly doted. He dwelt here apart from the world, seldom going out of doors and rarely receiving a visitor, if we except Ben Hanlon—a sort of half farmer, half bailiff—who worked the land retained by the squire, and collected the rents of those portions let to tenants, exercising at the same time a general surveillance over them all. This surveillance was accompanied by an amount of meddling and innumerable acts of petty tyranny which had earned for him the dislike, if not the hatred, of the whole tenantry, by whom he was invariably called "Black Ben."

The squire owned a considerable stretch of land. The greater part of this land had been let off in small farms of from seven to twenty acres. It had been so when he came into possession, and it so remained. Times without number had he been importuned by his agent to turn out of doors some unlucky or improvident tenant whose rent was in arrear, but the squire, either through indulgence or indolence, turned a deaf ear to Black Ben, or put him off with the remark, "Give them a little longer."

"Weel, squire, it'll jest be the langer the waur; the deil tae pye an' naethin' tae dae't wi'; hoonaniver, A suppose ye ken best, but yer no till blame me in the lang run," with which deliverance Ben would retire to his own quarters, grumbling as he went, but determined in the end to carry out matters after his own fashion.

The squire's property could boast of but few comfortable farmhouses. They were chiefly of the cottier class, bearing, oddly enough, a striking resemblance to the "Big Hoose" so far as cheerlessness and lack of comfort were concerned. There was one exception, however, and the very squalor and negligence visible in and around all the other dwellings, made the neat, tidy cottage of Widow Hunter stand out all the more in pleasing and striking contrast. The dwelling house faced the cart-road already referred to, standing back from it some twenty yards. The intervening space had been converted into a garden with neat hedgerows running along either side. It was too large a space, though, to be entirely devoted to the culture of flowers. That portion nearest the house was laid out in tiny patches, and planted with such horticultural specimens as the widow had been able to procure through the kindness of a neighbouring gardener. The remainder of the plot was devoted to the less ornamental but more profitable produce of early potatoes, beans, peas, and cabbage, flanked and intersected by rows of currant and gooseberry bushes. At right angles with the cottage, and towards the rere, stood the office houses, comprising stable, barn, byre, and piggery. These were built of stone and lime, with thatched roofs, and were in excellent repair. The dwelling-house was of the usual build, four plain whitewashed walls enclosing an oblong space, one story in height, surmounted by the inevitable thatched roof, and divided into three apartments—kitchen, bedroom, and parlour. Each apartment had but one window in front, small, but clean and unbroken; the wood-work painted white and forming a pleasant contrast with the door and its frame-work, which were of a bright fresh green.

The exterior was but an index to the interior. The earthen floor was scrupulously clean; the furniture was meagre but substantial; a large press standing against one wall held the family wardrobe; an old-fashioned mahogany chest of drawers with sloping top and bright brass knobs; a stout oaken table and capacious armchair, furnished another side of the kitchen, while a plain wooden "settlebed," painted brown, was placed against the third side. A corner cupboard, after the old style, with glass doors may be said to have completed the furnishing. The fourth side was occupied by the fireplace, which was one of the good old days. No polished grate or modern stove stood there, but upon the hearth, paved with round hard stones, blazed a cheerful turf fire, its ruddy glare reflected from the polished hoops of the churn and from the shining tins and lids of cans which hung upon the walls. From the cross-beams supporting the roof were suspended some home-cured hams and flitches of bacon, which in no way detracted from the homely aspect of the place.

WIDOW HUNTER

But Widow Hunter did everything well, and the house belongings seemed to reflect the good nature which shone from her eyes and beamed upon her happy, contented face. She was beloved by all with whom she came in contact, and her cheery words and charitable actions had endeared her to many of her less prosperous neighbours.

John Hunter had died leaving her a widow five years before the opening of my story. They had but one child, a son, now in his twenty-first year, the fine strapping fellow with whom my readers are already acquainted. At first the widow had despaired of being able to hold the farm, but when the seed time came John Stewart sent a plough and Sam Poag sent his horse, and Davey Thompson and John Kaig and other willing hands lent their aid, unasked, and in their own blunt kindly fashion. And so, year by year the seed was planted and the harvest was reaped; and now her son, young Johnnie Hunter, could hold a plough almost as well as his good father before him, and with a little assistance, still cheerfully given, the farm was worked to the best advantage.

But, alas! dark days were in store for the good-hearted Widow Hunter.

CHAPTER IV

BLACK BEN'S PROPOSAL

IT was the night of the Carrowdore ball. Widow Hunter had assisted her son to don his Sunday attire for the occasion, and had seen him off, with the request that he would not stay away all night. And Johnnie had told her not to sit up for him, but to lock the door and go to bed, leaving the key in its accustomed place. This was upon the window-sill—passing it out from the bedroom—where it was concealed by the leaves of a spreading rose bush growing at the spot.

And now the widow was alone. The door was barred and the window-blind unrolled. A huge peat fire burnt brightly on the hearth, its ruddy glare reflected from the tinware on the walls. Idleness was a thing unknown to the widow, and she was now busily engaged in baking homely bread. On a griddle, suspended over a bright red fire, were several wheaten bannocks, and numerous "farls" of sweet oat-cake were propped against a row of turf in front of the fire. With her snowy cap and spotless apron, her bright eye and cheerful good-looking face, the widow was by no means unattractive. She was still in the prime of life and "stood her age well." It was whispered by the neighbouring gossips that more than once she had been approached with offers of marriage, but that she had determined never again to wed. Looking at her in the mingled light of lamp and turf-fire as she bustles about the kitchen, now turning her bannocks and oat-cakes, and anon kneading out fresh ones upon the bakeboard, crooning all the while a verse of some well-known song—one is not surprised that some of the unwedded farmers should have sought her for his wife.

One man there was who had set his heart upon possessing

BLACK BEN'S PROPOSAL

her. It was Black Ben. She was not, however, aware of this. She had always received Ben at her house as she did other people—with a frank, kindly salutation and a cheery smile. And Ben's visits, too, were not unfrequent. Sometimes it occurred to the widow that he was playing the spy, so trivial were the excuses he made for dropping in. No sooner had he gone, however, than she would dismiss the subject from her mind. And yet Ben really liked her, though he had not as yet ventured to speak to her on the subject. The widow's kindly nature had thawed even the icy affections of Ben the bailiff, and at length he resolved upon speaking out. Thus stood matters at this stage of my story.

A rough-haired terrier dog lay at some distance from the fire, apparently asleep. Suddenly he leaped up and uttered a series of short, sharp barks. The widow paused in her work to look at him.

"What ails ye, Towser?" she asked. "Lie doon man, there's naething to disturb ye shair."

But the dog's sense of hearing was sharper than the widow's. He ceased barking at her command, but he faced the door as if ready to spring on some intruder. The next moment a step sounded on the gravelled path, and a hand was laid upon the latch. The door was barred.

"Wha's there?" asked the widow.

"It's me, Mistress Hunter," was the answer, in the harsh, guttural tones of Ben the bailiff.

Wondering what errand he now came upon, she withdrew the wooden bar, and Ben stepped in. He was a man of middle height, stoutly built, and awkward in his gait. He wore huge heavy boots, a suit of coarse frieze, and always carried a heavy stick. His hair and beard were black and shaggy, his brows knitted and overhanging, while his small cunning eyes, heavy jaws and coarse thick lips, formed a physiognomy the reverse of prepossessing.

He did not wait the invitation of the widow to be seated, but, striding towards the fire, placed himself in the arm chair, while Towser slunk off, growling deeply, and lay down in the corner.

"An' what way ir ye the nicht, Mistress Hunter?" asked Ben.

"Deed A daurnae compleen, Guid be thankit," said the widow; "it's freezin' gie an' keen A'm thinkin'."

"Sang, it is that, mem; A wudnae be surprised if we had a lang spell o't noo."

"Weel, weel, Ben; Providence kens what's best."

Ben did not answer, but sat staring into the fire for at least a minute. Then he looked up—

"Whaur's Johnnie?" he asked.

"Why whaur wud he be, dae ye think?" she replied, laughing; "whaur but at the dance in Carrowdore."

"A think he gangs to a guid wheen things o' that soart." said Ben.

"Agh, weel, the waen maun hae sumthing to amuse him; he's a guid boy an' warks hard an' sair, an' if he niver diz waur nor that it'll be weel fur him," and as she said this there was a look of motherly pride in her eye.

"Sae be it; sae be it." said the bailiff, "but A see nae guid in sich things."

"A dinna see the herm," was the somewhat warm reply; "mony a dance A went till myself; an' ye ken this yin's fur puir auld Corney O'Neill, the crayter."

"That auld wasp!" growled Ben, his brows knitting; "he's a country's pest, an' it's time he wuz oot o' the road."

"Agh puir buddy, it's a peety o' him," murmured the kindly woman; "his time canna be very lang noo."

"Weel, weel, let that flee stick tae the wa' jest noo," replied Ben; "A hae sumthin' else tae speak tae ye aboot."

Struck by the seriousness of the man's tones, Mrs. Hunter turned from her bakeboard, and, dusting the flour from her hands inquired—

"An' what may that be?"

"A hae been thinkin'," said Ben, "that ye wud be the better o' sum yin tae tak cherge o' this bit pert fur ye."

Scarcely comprehending the purport of this remark, the widow replied that she had nothing to complain of; her son worked hard, and the neighbours were kind, giving her a day's labour now and then ungrudgingly.

"Very true," said the bailiff, "but if A'm no' mistaken ye'll only hae Johnnie fur a short time, an' there's nae use o' ye been behauden till yer neibours."

"What maks ye say A'll no' hae Johnnie lang?" asked the widow, in a voice somewhat tremulous,

"Because he's gie an' affen at The Hill," said Ben; "an' he's no gaun there fur naethin'. He'll merry yin o' them bonnie lasses some day, an' gang hame tae the fether-in-law tae wark for him."

"Oh, weel," said the widow, stooping to turn her oaten cakes so that she might hide the look of anxiety which she felt must be plainly indicated upon her face, "Oh, weel, if its for his guid A'll no object; A hae been able tae wrasle through sae far, an' Providence wull no desert me in my auld days."

"Hoots, wuman!" said Ben, in a bantering tone, "dinnae talk aboot yer auld days; yer a young, fresh wuman yet; why there's no a grey hair in yer heid."

The widow did not reply. Turning to her table, she was about to resume her work when Ben said—

"Sit doon fur a bit, Mistress Hunter. A tell't ye A had sumthin' tae say till ye."

"Yer no fur risin' the rent A hope," remarked the widow, as she sat down on a chair, and shook the flour from her apron.

"That wull cum some day, but you hae a freen that'll no let muckle o' a rise gang on your bit lan'," said Ben.

"An' wha micht that be?" asked Mrs. Hunter.

"Jest mysel'," answered Ben; "tae tell ye the truth, Mistress,

A hae been takin' mair interest in yer affairs this while back than ye hae ony notion o' an' mony a thocht A hae had fur yer weelfare. In fact, tae pit twunty wurds intil yin, A want tae merry ye, Mistress Hunter."

The explosion of a thunderbolt in that homely little kitchen could not have startled Mrs. Hunter more than did that declaration by Ben in his usual cold, harsh and deliberate tones. She gave no reply. Indeed, she could not. So suddenly had the proposal come upon her that she felt dumbfounded. The feeling, however, passed off in a moment, and was succeeded by indignation. A warm flush mantled cheek and brow as she said, in a voice that trembled not a little.

"If that was what brocht ye here the nicht ye micht a saved yersel' the journey."

It was now Ben's turn to be amazed. Not for a single instant did he anticipate being directly rejected, and he could not now believe that he was unsuccessful, though the look and voice of the widow plainly betokened it. There was an awkward pause. Then Mrs. Hunter rose and resumed her household work.

"A'm sayin', Mistress Hunter," said Ben, "ye needna tak' me that short; cum an' talk the metter ower, in a raisonable menner."

"A'll no hear another wurd on the subject," said the widow, as she lifted a goose wing and deftly swept the bakeboard.

"Dinnae be ower rash," said Ben; "A hae a nice doon-sittin' for ye: twa guid horses, six kye, a wheen o' as fine pigs as iver ye clappit an e'e on; A hae the best powltry in the toonland, an' mony a yin wud like tae hae a guid thirty acre o' lan'."

He paused; but the enumeration of his possessions had no effect upon the widow, so he resumed.

"Your bit lan' merches mine, an' whun A'm here tae luk efter things ye'll no hae tae bother yer heid wi' ether Johnnie or yer neibours. Cum, noo, what dae ye say?"

"A hae this tae say," burst from the woman, as she faced round suddenly, "A hae this tae say, that A hae seen nae man fit to tak the place o' him that it was God's wull tae tak tae Himsel. A'll muckle change my min' if iver A tak onybody, but A wudnae be tied tae the like o' *you*, na, no' if every hair in yer heid had a goolden guinea at it."

"What fur?" asked Ben, as he rose and attempted to take the widow's hand. She drew back suddenly, and retiring as far from him as the furniture in that part of the kitchen would allow, she replied—

"Dinna ax me ony questions, an' dinna offer to pit yer han' on me! Ye hae insulted me enough a'reddy!"

"Hoo hae A insulted ye?" asked Ben, in a tone of surprise.

"Ye ken that athoot axin," said the widow. There was a pause, and then she added—"A maun get on wi' my work, an' A'm no wantin' ony company."

A frown gathered upon the dark, repulsive face of Ben. He stood for fully a minute looking sullenly into the fire; then he raised his eyes to the widow and said—

"Ye'll wush ye had taen me."

She did not answer; neither did she turn to look at him. He waited for another minute, then went towards the door, opened it, and, stepping out, closed it after him, without another word. When he reached the road, he turned and looked back. His black heart swelled with rage and failure, and he cursed himself for being befooled, as he phrased it, by a good-looking widow. Then he shook his clenched fist in the direction of the house and swore a terrible oath that he would be revenged.

And Black Ben kept his word.

CHAPTER V

AN AWKWARD FIX

WE left our young lovers in rather an awkward fix. What Jeannie had stated was quite true. They were tied in! The practice was then and still is a common one. The lovers had been followed at some distance by certain boys who envied Hunter and Taylor their popularity at "The Hill," and they indulged in a practical joke at their expense. The stout crossbar of a roadside gate was adroitly whipped off, and one of the fellows, stealing up to the house, quietly placed the piece of wood with one end upon the door step. The other end reached considerably above the top of the door-frame. Then taking a piece of stout cord from his pocket, he lashed the handle of the door-latch to the gate-bar, and the work was complete. To open the door from within was impossible, and then the boys slipped off, chuckling at the success of their joke.

No sooner had Jeannie made her whispered announcement to her companions than the position of affairs became instantly apparent. The young men must be concealed! But where? Necessity is the mother of invention, and the quick wit of the girls solved the difficulty. At a sign from Jeannie, Johnnie rolled himself under the sofa, while "the mester" crept into a churn which lay upon its side on the floor. This was the work of but a few seconds, and the next moment, Mrs. Banks, partially dressed and candle in hand, stalked into the room.

"What ir ye aboot, waen?" she asked, "why irn't ye in bed?" and she glanced round the apartment suspiciously.

"We hae jist din eatin' a peece breid an' butter," said Jeannie, thus skilfully evading the interrogation; "A suppose ye heerd Mary Ann an' me lauchin' aboot the fun we had. A declare, ma, but it was the pleesintest perty iver A wus at in my life."

As she spoke, the girls both left the room, preceded by their mother. By a little manoeuvring, Jeannie managed to get left behind for a moment in the kitchen. Gliding swiftly and silently back into the room she whispered in the hearing of Johnnie.

"A wudnae for the wurl my ma seen ye here. Ye maun stae a' nicht an' A'll manage tae get ye oot in the mornin'."

"Cum awa', Jeannie!" cried the mother in sharp tones, and Jeannie retreated from the room to retire to bed in no very pleasant frame of mind.

But the case of the boys was one more serious by far. Johnnie lay, face downwards, upon a cold earthen floor; while young Taylor, sticking head foremost in the churn, was almost suffocated. Unwilling to compromise the young ladies, and realising the necessity of preserving absolute silence until the old lady had settled down for the night, they lay for fully ten minutes without stirring. At the end of that period, which though brief seemed to the imprisoned ones like hours, an incident occurred which well-nigh led to their discovery. A soft pattering noise was heard upon the earthen floor, accompanied by the sound of some animal sniffing. It was the dog! Now this brute was an intelligent one, and knew both Taylor and Hunter by sight, but his instinct plainly disclosed to him the presence of strangers in that particular apartment, and it was but natural to suppose that should the dog discover them in hiding—which he was certain to do—he might make his company somewhat unpleasant. This thought flashed simultaneously through the minds of the young men as they lay, scarcely daring to breathe. Hunter was nearest to the door, and his heart beat wildly as he heard the big brute sniffing about the end of the sofa. Suddenly a happy thought struck him. When about to take his departure, Jeannie had insisted upon stuffing into his coat pocket two large slices of bread and butter. "Good, kind girl!"

he mentally exclaimed, as with some difficulty he managed to draw the bread and butter from his pocket and gently push it in the direction of the dog's nose. The bait took; "Captain" speedily demolished the tempting morsel, and pushing his head under the sofa uttered a subdued whine. Hunter continued to stroke its head, and whispered, soothingly—"Poor fellow! Poor Captain!"

Thus might all have gone well, but just at that moment Taylor was seized with an irresistible desire to sneeze. He struggled hard to avoid it, but in vain. It would come, and come it did! "Captain" uttered a low growl, and sprang in the direction from which the sound proceeded. The next instant he had seized Taylor by the leg. Flesh and blood could stand it no longer, and Taylor, letting out with his other leg, gave the dog a tremendous kick, which forced him to let go and bark furiously. The hubbub in an instant was terrific. Hunter and Taylor crept from their concealment, and the dog, evidently terrified, bounded into the kitchen, barking with all his might.

"The deil choke it!" muttered Hunter.

Then voices were heard from the upper bedrooms. Jeannie was overheard assuring her mother that "the dug wuz chasin' that strange cat again," and then Banks himself, roused by the noise, cried in a loud voice—

"Chew, sir; awa' an' lie doon, Captain!"

With a sullen growl Captain obeyed, and Hunter, to guard against further intrusion, closed the room door. Neither of the young men ventured to speak for some time; then, in cautious whispers they held a consultation.

"Did he hurt ye?" asked Hunter.

"Not much," answered Taylor; "the leg of my boot saved me. Captain got the worst of it."

"Bad luck till him!" muttered the other; "but A'm sayin', Mester, we maun get oot o' this."

"But how?" queried the master.

"A'll try the wundey efter a bit," whispered Hunter. "It's no the first time A hae cum in through it an' A dinnae see why we cudnae gang oot by it."

"But they may hear us," said Taylor.

"We'll chance it whun A think they're asleep," said Hunter. "We're shair tae be catched if we stae a' nicht." Then he added with a quiet chuckle—"Jeannie keeps the wundey frame weel creeshed fur me onywae."

To this proposal Taylor readily agreed, for he was seriously anxious and weary. He had gone there for the sole purpose of obliging Hunter, and to be found secreted in the house would have been to him very unpleasant. Side by side they sat for nearly an hour, scarcely daring to exchange even a whisper.

"A'll try it noo," said Hunter, as he crept cautiously towards the window. Both had removed their boots, which they carried in their hands. The "catch" was silently undone, and the lower half of the window was pushed up noiselessly. Hunter held it thus while Taylor crept out—a very simple matter as the window sill was not a couple of feet from the ground. Taylor performed a like office for Hunter; the latter slipped down the window with all possible caution; then both glided off like spectres. Five minutes afterwards, with their boots replaced, they were trudging along the highway, laughing heartily at their adventure.

"Now, look here, Johnnie," said Taylor, "never ask me to go in there again at night, for I won't do it."

Johnnie laughed.

"Man that's naethin'!" said he; "mony a time A hae been oot the hale blissid nicht. Did iver A tell ye what happened Sammy Reid an' me?"

"No, Johnnie; what was that?"

"Weel, Sammy wuz a guid dale aulder nor me, but we fell in thegither at the last Hervest Fair in Newtown, an' sez Sammy tae me, sez he, 'A hae a guid thing on, but A want company. Wull ye gang?' A said A wud, an' we went hame wi' twa as nice lasses as ye wud wush tae clap an e'e on. But lo-and-behold-ye didn't it come on the maist sayries spate o' rain that nicht that iver A seen. It was judgment like, and fur three days an' nichts it niver slackit."

"And what did you do?" asked Taylor.

"What cud we dae, Mester? A jist had to stay whaur A wuz."

"Of course Sammy stayed with you."

"He did, an' mony a guid lauch A had at him. Whun we were comin' back hame, sez he 'Johnnie, ye'll no grup me bein' sich a fool again. A'm jest skunnered wi' coortin', so A em!'"

"Well, Johnnie, I'm pretty much in the same condition. Why don't you go and court Jeannie in the day time?"

"It's easy for ye tae talk," replied Hunter; "A wush her auld mither wuz deid; why can't she let a buddy gang back an' forrit like ither fowk?"

"I confess, Johnnie," said the master, "that while there may be a tinge of romance and fascination about these nocturnal expeditions, I can't altogether reconcile my mind to them."

"What dae ye mean by *nocturnal?*" queried Hunter.

"I mean by night," said Taylor, laughing.

"Weel A wush ye wudnae pit in them jawbrekers whun yer talkin' till me," said Hunter. "Hooaniver, mester, there's no yin bit herm in it; but efter a' if A cud get sittin' crackin' the wae A want wi' Jeannie afore her fowk A wudnae ax tae be there at nicht. Luk at John Gordon there—or the doctor as we ca' him—he aye sits and reads the paper when Rabert M'Kay gangs in tae coort his dochtor."

"That's very considerate of him," said Taylor.

"Aye, but the fun o' it is," continued Hunter, laughing, "that the buddy cannae read yin bit; hooaniver he purtends he can, an' ye wud niver dee another daith if ye heerd his mistress sayin' tae the waens—'Haud yer tongues, wull ye, and let yer da read the paper!'"

"Johnnie, you'll kill me with laughing at your stories," said Taylor; "but tell me, how much did you get for old Corney?"

"Jest fifty shillin'."

"I expected more."

"Ay, there shud a been twice that, but there wuz a sayrious lot o' whuskey drunk. It wud pye Mistress Punton o' Carrowdore, and Boyd o' Greyab,* gie an' weel. Fitty M'Cormick had tae gang for anither gallon."

Taylor laughed. "What odd names you have for people here," he said. "Sure 'Fitty' can't be any man's name?"

"He niver gets ocht else," said Hunter. "It's because he walks quer; ivery step he taks he knocks yin fut up against the tither heel. Some fowk starts nicknames on theirsels. We ca' yin man 'See-luk-see'; and John Cleland ca's Harper O'Cardy 'Donegall Cherley.'"

"Are the people not offended at such names being applied to them?" asked the master.

"Na, no yin bit," said Hunter; "A think some fowk likes them. But A wuz talkin' aboot the whuskey. Ye micht as weel throw it on a bag o' chaff as doon sum o' thon boys' throats. An' as for cheese. A think sum o' the fellows ocht tae be seeck. They'll be like the man frae Ballyboley that got the feed o' cheese an' porter. Did iver A tell ye that, mester?"

"You did, Johnnie, and for goodness sake don't tell it to me again."

"Weel, did A tell ye aboot Mary Deans at the Carrowdore suree?"

"You did; and very cruel it was to stuff the creature in such a fashion."

---

* Greyabbey.

"Stuff her!" exclaimed Johnnie; "man ye cudnae dae her ony herm. They say that Carmichael's mills at Millisle cudnae keep her in meal and flooer."

"And did she really drink twenty cups of tea at the Carrowdore soiree?" asked the schoolmaster.

"Ay, man, she did; an' then yin o' the boys gied her a cup o' kofay, an' she said the tay was gettin' the langer the better. She never kent the difference. But tell me, Mester, wull we gie Corney the money, or wull we buy him sumthin's wi' it?"

"Better to tell him how much we have raised, and consult him as to what we shall do with it."

Thus did the young men converse as they travelled mile after mile, for their journey was not a short one. Now and then the schoolmaster was compelled to stop, so heartily did he laugh at the stories told by Hunter, many of which, if here reproduced, would be well known all over the broad Ards. Taylor's lodgings were situate about five minutes' walk from Hunter's home, and when the former had been reached, the young men shook hands and said good-night. It was arranged that Taylor should visit Corney O'Neill on the following day after school hours and communicate to the old man the pleasing intelligence that he was the possessor of the princely sum of fifty shillings! Taylor kept his engagement, and he was not a moment too soon.

CHAPTER VI

CORNEY O'NEILL

AT no great distance from Widow Hunter's farm stood a wretched hovel. It would be more accurate to say the ruins of a hovel, for of the two rooms of which it had originally consisted one had fallen down. The gable of what remained was bulged out and seemed in imminent danger of giving way at any moment. A stout branch of a tree, one end stuck into the ground, the other placed against the gable, served as a prop to prevent the wall from falling. The thatched roof, or so much of it as remained, was grown over with moss and weeds, and the chimney had been blown away entirely. There was but one window; it was about eighteen inches square and fitted with small diamond-shaped panes of glass, not one of which was intact. A few were entirely demolished, and their places supplied by paper, straw, and rags.

The interior was not more inviting. The walls and rafters were begrimed with smoke. A heap of straw, lying in a corner, covered partly by the remains of an old quilt, was the only indication of a bed. A small, rickety table, two four-legged stools and a couple of large flat stones for seats, a broken pot, a few cracked plates and dishes, a terribly blackened, battered teapot, and an old griddle were the sole equipments of the place.

And yet it was a human habitation! In this miserable hut lived Corney O'Neill, for sixty years a faithful servant upon Squire Brown's property, and the squire's own factotum until old age and declining health rendered him unfit for even the lightest labour. Squire Brown would not hear of him being sent to the poorhouse, and at Corney's request gave him permission to remain in the old house where he had been born. Corney was alone in the world so far as relatives were concerned, but the kind-hearted neighbours supplied his wants, which were few. A little tobacco and tea, a few potatoes and an occasional handful of meal were never missed, and the old man's end could not be far off. For a good while the squire had sent him regular supplies of milk, potatoes, and meal; but these gradually dropped off. Some said Black Ben was to blame for the oversight, but as time wore on the subject was seldom referred to, and in all probability the squire was in utter ignorance even of the fact of the old man's existence.

Corney O'Neill was eighty years of age. He looked much older. Hard work and constant exposure to all kinds of weather had told upon his once sturdy frame, and as he now sat upon one of the large flat stones, his body bent forward and his large, skinny hands extended over the embers of the broken branches and chips of wood that smouldered upon the hearth, he was a picture the contemplation of which would have excited the pity and sympathy of even the most casual beholder. His beard and the few straggling locks of hair upon his head were white as snow. His eyes were sunken and lustreless, his face pinched, pale and wrinkled.

On the evening after the Carrowdore punch ball, Corney sat in his favourite attitude by his scanty fire. His head inclined forward; his hands were spread out; his eyes fixed intently on the glowing embers. Now and then he would rub his hands gently together and his lips would move as though he conversed with himself, but no sound came forth. Once or twice he had turned partly round to replenish the fire from a heap of broken sticks and dried whins piled in the corner by some thoughtful neighbours. This done he would relapse into the same mood as before.

Corney was a remarkable man. In his time he was a gay, cheery fellow, and a favourite with all who knew him. He married when about fifty. One child was born to him, a boy, who grew up a strapping young fellow, the pride of his parents' hearts. Country life and its occupations were too monotonous for young Harry O'Neill's restless spirit, and so when one fine morning he started off to dispose of a couple of young pigs in the Newtownards market, he made up his mind to go and push his fortune. He sold his pigs, sent a message by Pattie Kaig to his father that some day he would return and give him the price of the pigs; but from that day he was never heard of more. His mother died two years after his departure, and from that hour Corney was an altered man. Silent and gloomy, he pursued his daily avocations as carefully and as efficiently as ever; but his spirit had received its death blow, and though the body lived the spirit seemed utterly blighted. Then his health broke down and his working days were at an end. Several of the country folk had offered him a home; but he preferred to spend the remainder of his life in solitude within the walls where he had first opened his eyes, and which had contained all that was dear to him in this world.

As Corney sat warming himself on the evening of which I write, he heard a step approaching the door; the latch was lifted, the door pushed open, and Black Ben entered.

Corney did not look up. He took it to be one of the neighbours who passed out and in and who, knowing his habits, unless he addressed them, usually left without speaking a word.

Ben closed the door behind him, stepped into the middle of the floor and looked around. It was only a hurried glance. Then he fixed his eye upon Corney, and watched him closely. He appeared to have something on his mind which he wished to say and yet felt a reluctance to speak. Something in the aspect of that frail, old creature, so near to the confines of another world, seemed to awe him. It was only for a moment. The old, hard look came into his eyes and settled about his mouth, and the old harsh tone came into his voice as he said:—

"Weel, Corney, so yer here yit!"

The old man startled and passed a trembling hand across his eyes. Then he turned slowly round upon his seat, and in a weak shaky voice replied:—

"Ay, Ben; here still, but it'll no be lang; it'll no be lang noo."

"Ye hae kept tellin' me that ower lang, Corney, an' A'll be put aff nae mair. If ye dinna cleer oot by twal o'clock the morrow, A'll throw ye intil the dyke shugh wi' my ain han's." Corney's head dropped slowly forward until it rested upon his knees. Thus he sat without speaking, but his lips moved and his fingers were clutched convulsively.

"Dae ye heer me, Corney?" asked Ben gruffly.

"A dae, A dae," was the feeble response.

"Weel, min' A'll no be put aff this time; A hae put up wi' ye till A'm tired, an' the auld wa's maun cum doon oot o' this."

Corney lifted his head and a pleading look crept into his sunken eyes. Then he said—

. "Mester Ben, Mester Ben, a wheen days wull finish it noo. Let me dee whaur A em an' no bother the neibors. Whun A'm laid doon bye, aside my puir Nancy, the auld hoose wull no' be hard to pu' doon."

"There's plenty o' the neibors wul take ye in an' keep ye," growled Ben.

"A'll no bother them; it's no' worth while," said Corney, and again his head slid forward upon his knees.

Ben was fast losing his temper. He was about to speak, but checked himself, and going to the door looked out. Then he stepped back and half whispered, half muttered into the old man's ear—

"Mind what A say, Corney, A'll be here at twal o'clock the morrow and if A get ye here—."

He stopped and looked up as a shadow fell upon the floor.

The schoolmaster stood in the open door. Black Ben did not finish his sentence. Drawing his hat down over his brow, and with an angry look in his eyes, he passed out of the hut without speaking to the young man who was evidently about to address him.

CHAPTER VII

A FRIEND IN NEED

THE schoolmaster stood upon the damp earthen floor of Corney O'Neill's wretched dwelling for several minutes before the old man was aware of his presence. With the cruel words of Ben the bailiff still ringing in his ears the poor old creature sat with his hands covering his face, and the big, salt tears dropping between his fingers. At length Taylor placed his hand gently on the old man's shoulders, and, in a soft, kindly voice said—

"Corney!"

The man started and looked up.

"Ah, mester, is it you?" he said. "A thocht Black Ben was there a' the time."

"He went out as I came in," said the schoolmaster.

Corney sat some moments silent. Then he turned partly round toward Taylor, and raising his weak, trembling, skinny hands over his head, while he turned his almost sightless orbs towards the blackened rafters of his hut, he said, in a voice that was hollow and unnatural—

"*Mester, that man wull niver dee in his bed!*"

"Why, Corney?" asked Taylor.

"Acause he afflicts and persecutes the puir and helpless," said Corney.

"Has he been annoying you?" asked Taylor.

For fully a minute the old man sat moaning, while his hand wandered aimlessly about over his face and scanty locks.

"Annoyin' me," at length he groaned; "he haes niver din wi' that, mester. There's rent due on these auld wa's, an' he says he'll throw me oot at twal o'clock the morrow if it's no pied. It wudna be lang he wud hae to wait, mester, fur A'm din, cleen din; but it's hard to be throwed out in the dyke-sheugh."

"Can a man be so cruel?" said the teacher, while a flush of honest indignation mantled his cheek and brow. "How much is due, Corney, and I'll see if it can't be paid?"

"A dinna ken, mester; A dinna ken; but it canna be terble muckle. Shairly the squire, that A served sae lang an' weel, kens naethin' o' this or he wudna heer o' it."

Taylor drew from his pocket a great handful of money; coppers, sixpences, and shillings, with here and there an odd half-crown.

"Look here, Corney!" he exclaimed; "fifty shillings, and all yours."

Corney turned his dim and all but sightless orbs in the direction of the master's voice.

"Fifty shillin'!" he murmured, "fifty shillin' and a' mine; wha sent me that, mester?"

"We earned it for you at the dance last night, Corney. Although Ben the bailiff treats you harshly you have friends who will not see you wronged."

Corney's head dropped upon his knees, and tears—this time of gratitude—fell plentifully from his aged eyes.

"Come, Corney, cheer up!" said Taylor, briskly; "see, I'll put this money here in this bowl for you; and look, Corney, here's a drop of something that your friend, James Boyd, of Greyabbey, sent you to warm your old heart and drink his health in."

As he spoke he drew a bottle from his pocket and looked about him for a glass. There was none, but a cracked teacup served as a substitute. Pouring out a small quantity of the liquor he diluted it with water from an old tin can, and handed it to Corney.

"Is it whiskey?" enquired Corney; "ah, mester dear, Mister Boyd's a dacent man."

"He is, Corney," replied Taylor, "and you'll find that will do you good. It's a drop of old Irish whiskey—good as gold, Corney, for a weak heart. I don't approve of the free use of strong drink, but there are times when it is beneficial. Drink it off, Corney."

With a trembling hand the old creature raised the teacup and drained the contents. Almost instantly the potent spirit mounted to his weak brain, and the effect was marvellous. He smiled; rubbed his hands, then clapped them and laughed—a weak, peculiar, chuckling laugh.

"Ay, mester, it's usefu'," he said, "there maun be sumthin' in it; did ye iver hear what Andy Moreland said?" and he looked up with a momentary sparkle in his eyes.

"No, Corney, what was it?"

"Major Crawford axed him yince waz he a teetotaller. 'Na,' says Andy, 'A haenae been a teetotaller for mair nor foarty year; whun we cum intil the wurl the meedwife wats oor lips wi' whuskey, an' whun we're deein, an' no fit tae dae ocht fur oorsels, the doctor pits a wee drap doon oor throats. There maun be guid in it,' says Andy."

And the frail old creature chuckled over his joke.

"Now, Corney, I must leave you," said Taylor; "but tell me, do you think Ben means to turn you out to-morrow?"

"As shair as A'm sittin' here, mester, A believe he wull," said Corney, his momentary exhilaration passing off, and the old look settling upon his pale and pinched face.

"Well, Corney, give yourself no concern or trouble about the matter. Did you ever know me to break my word?"

"Niver, mester," replied Corney, eagerly.

"Well, listen to me, Corney; at twelve o'clock to-morrow there will be those here who will protect you; and if Black Ben attempts to carry out his threat let him look to himself! Goodbye, Corney."

"Guid-bye, mester; God will bliss ye fur yer kindness tae me."

The old man settled down into his accustomed attitude, and Taylor, with a moistened eye, quietly withdrew, closing the door softly behind him.

"And now for Hunter's," he muttered, as he clenched his teeth. "He can get the whole country to muster, if necessary, and if Ben dares to disturb that wretched old creature, let him look to himself, that's all!"

CHAPTER VIII

A CONSULTATION

A BRISK walk over the crisp, frost-bound road soon brought Taylor to Widow Hunter's. As he opened the door and stepped inside, the dog leaped upon him, barking a joyous welcome; Johnnie saluted him with a cheery, "Morrow, mester, jist in time for yer tay"; and Mrs. Hunter bustled from the adjoining apartment to hand him a chair and enquire "wuz there ocht new?"

A cheerful picture did that homely kitchen present—a pleasing contrast to the habitation which Taylor had just left. It was tea time. In a broad frying pan, suspended from a crook over a bright turf fire, were some eggs, and a number of nice large slices of home-cured ham, hissing and sputtering. A small round table, with spotless white cover, stood near the fire, and on it were placed some old-fashioned cups and saucers, a heap of home-made bread and a print of sweet, fresh butter. The shining tin teapot was steaming hot as it stood on a red "peat-coal" crushed flat upon the hearth.

From her cupboard the widow fetched a cup and saucer for Taylor, saying, as she did so—

"A'm sae gled, sir, that ye jist happened in at the richt time; draw in yer chair if ye pleese; there's naething very temptin', but ye ken yer welkim tae it, sich as it is."

Taylor knew from experience that he need not decline the proffered hospitality; so, drawing a chair up to the little round table, he sat down. The ham and eggs were deftly tossed upon the various plates, the tea was poured out, creamed, and sugared, and then the widow took her place at the table.

"Noo, mester, yer nae stranger"; she said, in her kindly cheery

A CONSULTATION

tones; "so pit forrit yer han' an' tak' whativer ye fancy."

"I'll do that, Mrs. Hunter," said the schoolmaster.

"Ye niver tell me tae eat, ma," said Johnnie, laughing.

"Na, there's nae need for that, A'm thinkin'," said the widow; "but A like tae see folk takin' their meat, for a' that. A wud rather pye for guid meat than fur doctor's drugs."

"Did you see Corney?" asked Johnnie.

"I did," said the teacher. "He's in very low spirits."

"God help the crayter!" fervently ejaculated the widow; "it's a wonner tae me hoo he's leevin' ava; A hope he's no wantin' for ocht, mester."

"He seems to have food and fire, but he thinks his end is at hand," replied Taylor.

"A'm certain the buddy canna pit ower muckle langer," said Mrs. Hunter. "Doctor Woods, o' Bangor, wuz oot this road the tither day an' he spauk in the daur till me. He said he had lukid in tae see Corney, and that he thocht he wudnae leev lang."

"It wuz kin' o' Dokter Woods tae dae that," remarked Johnnie.

"Just what I would expect from his kindly heart," chimed in Taylor. "But Corney fears something more than death; he is in dread of being turned out of his miserable dwelling. Black Ben has sworn to fling him out to-morrow at twelve o'clock."

"A'm d—d if he wull!" exclaimed young Hunter, dropping his knife and fork and striking the table with his clenched fist till the tea utensils danced.

A look of sudden alarm settled upon the widow's face as she put down her cup.

"Johnnie, dinnae sweer dear," she said gently; "an' dinnae you interfere wi' Ben; he's a bad yin, an' wud be gled o' a chance agen you aboon a' ithers."

"A dinnae care for him the velye o' *that!*" said Johnnie, snapping his fingers; "dae ye think A'll stan' up an' see an auld dee'in man throwed oot agen the dyke side? Na, no if Ben wuz the heecht o' Scrabba muntin."*

"Keep oot o' truble, Johnnie; an' keep oot o' the law" urged the widow, who was becoming seriously distressed; then, with an effort to change the subject, she added, "cum waens, tak' yer tay; wull ye hae anither egg, mester."

"No, thank you, Mrs. Hunter."

"Wull you, Johnnie?"

"Na, A can eat nae mair; A'm jest chokin' wi' anger," said Johnnie.

"Noo, ye'll see there'll be naethin' o' it ava," said the widow; "nae man cud hae the heart tae dae ocht o' the soart. Shair they cudnae, mester?"

"Mrs. Hunter, I believe Black Ben to be capable of any cruelty," said Taylor. "He was in the act of leaving Corney's house as I entered, and the expression of his face was absolutely fiendish. I am determined to be at Corney's to-morrow at twelve o'clock, accompanied by some friends—."

"A'll be yin o' them," interrupted Johnnie.

"If any violence is attempted," continued Taylor, "I shall certainly interfere on behalf of the old man."

"Ye'll mebbe get into bother," said the widow; "what wud ye think o' callin' on the squire aboot it."

"That idea has occurred to me," answered Taylor; "but Ben is a cunning rascal. I am convinced the squire would not consent to the commission of so heartless an act, and when he would take Ben to task about it the fellow would deny his intentions. What I purpose doing is this: I shall be there to watch proceedings, and if Ben actually attempts to carry out his threat—."

"A'll smash his ugly face!" broke in Johnnie.

The widow wrung her hands.

"No need for that," said the master, laughing. "I shall caution

---

* Scrabo mountain.

A CONSULTATION

him to desist and shall send a deputation on the instant to Squire Brown to inform him of what is transpiring."

"That's the very thing," said the widow, somewhat relieved. "Waens, dear, dae naethin' rash."

Johnnie had risen and was walking about in a state of strong mental excitement. He was about to indulge in some forcible language, but noticing the distressed look upon his mother's face, he merely said—

"Wull ye cum oot, Mester?"

"Whaur ir ye gaun?" asked his mother quickly.

"Nae whaur," he replied, sullenly.

Taylor saw the position of affairs, and attempted to dissuade young Hunter from interfering. "There need be no violence," he said, "but if it should come to blows there will be some hard-fisted gentry there." Then with a look he cautioned Johnnie to be silent.

"Weel, weel, pleese yersel'," said the hot-headed youth.

The master did not remain much longer. The widow was evidently distressed, and Johnnie was not in a mood for conversation; so, picking up his stick and hat, Taylor bade his friends good-night and went away. He did not go home. He called upon some half-dozen of the tenantry for a purpose which my readers can doubtless divine.

Next day, between eleven and twelve o'clock, several sturdy farmers might have been observed going in the direction of Corney O'Neill's hut, where a scene was about to take place which, it is to be hoped, has had few, if any, parallels in prosperous Ards.

CHAPTER IX

AN EVICTION

THE schoolmaster was the first to reach Corney's dwelling. He found the old man sitting just as he had left him. "Well, Corney, I hope you had a good night's sleep," he said, cheerily.

"Na, mester; A had but a puir nicht o' it; an' twa or three times A thocht A seen *her*," said the old man, feebly.

"Saw whom or what?" asked Taylor.

"Nancy, my deid wife," mumbled Corney.

Taylor was about to make some remark, but just then Sam Stewart and Tom Gaw, two of the squire's tenantry, stepped in. Soon others arrived, some singly, others in pairs, until nearly twenty had mustered. Taylor, as we have said before, was very popular with the farmers in his district, and the lively interest taken by him in the welfare of Corney, raised him still higher in their estimation. He spoke to each man who arrived, and told them what course he suggested. He was to act as spokesman.

"Remember," he said, "let there be no violence if it can be avoided. I'll do the talking, and if a blow should be needed," he added, smiling, "I suppose some of you can attend to that."

"Jist lee that pert o' the wark tae me," said Sam Stewart, a big, broad shouldered fellow, with a fist that could have felled an ox.

"Ay, heth Sam, you can dae that," said several, and there was a laugh.

Just then three men were seen crossing the fields in the direction of Corney's hut. One of them was Black Ben; the others were dirty, greasy-looking fellows. They carried sticks, and belonged to the class called, by courtesy, "law messengers." Ben was not acting rashly; he had procured the necessary authority, and his act, however cruel, was *legal*.

AN EVICTION

As Ben stepped forward, followed by his two skulking attendants, he eyed the assembled tenantry with evident surprise; but assuming a careless, bantering tone, he said:—

"Weel, boys, have ye cum tae see a rat hunt?"

No one replied to the coarse, unfeeling jest, and Ben, with his two ruffians, stepped into the hut. Here there was another surprise for him. The schoolmaster and half a dozen farmers were standing on the floor. Without speaking to, or taking the slightest notice of them, Ben stepped up to old Corney, and placing his hand on his shoulder, said—

"Weel, Corney, ir ye reddy tae gang?"

Corney burst into tears, and there was a murmur amongst the farmers which foretold the coming storm.

"Parden me, Ben," said the schoolmaster; "how much does Corney owe you?"

"It's nane o' yer business," growled Ben; "if ye wur mindin' yer skule it wad be tellin' ye better."

"I do attend to my school, and do justice to the children entrusted to me," said Taylor.

"Ay, ye dae!" said Ben sneeringly. "Ye wud rether be galavantin' aboot the country wi' a gun unner yer erm."

"We can discuss that matter at some other time," replied Taylor; "but tell me, Ben, do you really mean to evict this poor creature? You must have some personal spleen against him. You can't mean to throw him out like a dog!"

"A'll suin show ye that," said Ben; "A hae had an *injectment* agen him this mony a day. It's no worth while haudin' an aukshen o' the furnitor," he added, looking round with a brutal laugh, "hooiniver Corney's bound tae budge this time."

"We are prepared to pay whatever rent is due," urged Taylor.

"Naebuddy axed ye fur rent," said Ben, "an' since ye appear tae hae sich a gra fur the auld man ye had better hoise him on yer back an' tak him hame wi' ye."

"Look here!" said Taylor, struggling to keep down his rising anger; "since you refuse to accept this offer understand how matters stand. We are here to protect Corney from this outrage. Dare not you nor your minions to touch one grey hair of that old man's head, or by Heaven you shall repent it. Squire Brown shall hear of your conduct; Squire Brown, whom Corney served for more than half a century; the old man was born within these walls; he has spent his whole life here, and his only wish is to die here. A few days may end his miserable existence, and you surely cannot be so cruel as to turn a dying man out of doors upon a cold winter's day."

Taylor was compelled to pause; there was a choking sensation in his throat, and for a few moments there was but one sound heard—the low, convulsive sobbing of old Corney.

Ben seemed to hesitate, but it was only for an instant. Turning to his assistants he pointed to Corney and simply said—

"*Carry him oot!*"

The fellows stepped nimbly one on each side of Corney to execute the order, but they were startled by the manly voice of Sam Stewart, who, stepping up to them, shouted—

"Touch him if ye daur! The first yin that pits a finger on him A'll fell him tae the grun'!"

The fellows slunk back, completely cowed.

"Blast ye!" shouted Ben, "A'll dae it mysel'," and he seized Corney by the shoulders.

But just as his unhallowed hands touched him, Sam dealt him a terrific blow in the face. It came straight from the shoulder and would have felled an ox. Ben went down with a crash.

Just then old Corney was observed to slip off the stone upon which he had been sitting, and fall upon the floor. Some of the men lifted him up tenderly, and placed him upon his seat. His head hung upon his breast.

"Get water some o' ye; he haes fainted!" cried one.

AN EVICTION

They raised the head of the old man, and bathed his white and ghastly face. But there was no sign of returning animation.

The eviction was no longer necessary.

Corney was dead!

A look of horror fell upon every face. Those who had been outside crowded in and stood looking on in speechless wonder. Corney was gently laid upon his bed of straw. Then Ben was looked to by his assistants.

"A doot ye hae killed him," said one of them, roughly.

But Ben was simply stunned, and the blood was flowing from his mouth and nose. His men assisted him to his feet and he revived. There was a dazed look upon his eye. He did not attempt to speak, and his men led him outside where they bathed his bleeding face. Then they told him what had happened, and he slunk away with a scared look, followed by his minions.

Meantime the farmers crowded around the dead body of Corney, in silence, horror-struck, and scarcely able to realise what had taken place. As they stood thus, mute and wondering, a female figure was observed at the door.

"The squire's dochtor, boys!" whispered one.

The next moment she entered and addressed them.

CHAPTER X

SQUIRE BROWN'S DAUGHTER

WIDOW HUNTER had but little sleep on the night of the schoolmaster's visit. Her heart, naturally kind, was touched with sympathy for the poor and unfortunate Corney O'Neill but that was not her chief concern. She had a foreboding that Black Ben would work her some evil. Her rejection of his suit would, she knew, rankle in his breast and make him eager to have revenge.

Her son was a hot-headed, impetuous youth, whose generous spirit could not brook such conduct as Ben was about to be guilty of. She felt certain that if Johnnie went to the eviction he would lose all control over himself, assault Ben, and probably be punished for it. All that night she tossed upon a sleepless pillow, and when she dropped off now and then into a fitful doze, Johnnie appeared before her in her dreams. Once she saw Ben creeping up behind to murder him, and she woke up with a loud scream. Again she saw her boy being led off by the police, handcuffed; at another time she saw him being drowned, and glad she was when the old clock struck six. Starting up she dressed quickly, and hurried to Johnnie's apartment to see that he was safe and sound.

At breakfast she extracted a promise from him that if he did go to Corney's he would simply be an eye-witness, and would not interfere in any way. Somewhat relieved by that promise, the widow set about her household duties but her mind was elsewhere. Suddenly she stopped in her work and sat down.

"That's the very thing," she said to herself; "A wunner it didnae strek me afore."

She looked at the clock; it was almost eleven.

"A hae jest time and nae mair," she continued, and then she bustled about, making preparations for a journey.

Her toilet arrangements did not occupy much time, and she was soon dressed. A warm woollen dress, Paisley shawl, straw bonnet of the good old type, and large gingham umbrella were her chief adornments, as she stepped out and locking her door placed the key in her pocket.

Mrs. Hunter walked straight to the "Big House," and knocked at the door. It was opened by the servant girl, who greeted the widow with a pleasant—

"What wae ir ye the day, mem?"

"Bravely, thank ye, Jane; is Miss Broon in the noo?"

"She is, mem; were ye wanting tae see her?"

"Jest fur a minit or twa if it wud be convaynient, Jane."

"Weel, jest cum in, mem, an' A'll tell her," said Jane.

Mrs. Hunter went in and sat down in the kitchen whilst Jane went in search of her young mistress. She had not long to wait. Jane returned in about a minute, and, asking Mrs. Hunter to follow her, she escorted her to Miss Brown's apartment.

I have already stated that Squire Brown was not childless. Annie Brown was his daughter, his only child, and he loved her dearly—she was the image of his dead wife—her mother. Somewhat under middle height, slender, but with faultless form, with a sweet, childish face, blue eyes, and a profusion of golden hair waving carelessly round her fair neck and shoulders in natural ringlets, Annie was what was termed in her neighbourhood "a doon richt beauty." She had but recently come home from a first-class boarding school, at which she had received an excellent education, and since her return had endeared herself to her father's tenantry by her gentle and unassuming manners.

Annie, from her very infancy, had known Mrs. Hunter, and she now met her with both hands extended in kindly greeting.

"Good morning, Mrs. Hunter," she exclaimed; "how very glad I am to see you."

"Thank ye, miss, thank ye," said the widow; "A shudnae bother ye sae early in the day."

"Don't talk of 'bother,' my dear Mrs. Hunter," said the charming girl. "Is there anything I can do for you, or do you wish to speak to papa?"

"There's bad work gaun on at Corney's, an' a thocht A shud cum an' tell ye aboot it," said the widow.

"What! at Corney O'Neill's?" exclaimed Annie, "whatever can it be?"

Mrs. Hunter told all she knew, and as she did so the tears gathered in the girl's blue eyes.

"Poor old Corney!" she said, "poor old man! He used to nurse me, Mrs. Hunter; and how I used to tease him in the garden, stealing the flowers and fruit of which he was so proud. Oh, Ben must be a bad man. I'm sure papa knows nothing of all this."

"Can ye dae ocht in the metter, mem," asked the widow, anxiously. "A'm feered sumthin' awful may happen." Annie looked at her watch.

"It is not yet twelve o'clock," she said, "and I may yet be in time. I shall go to Corney's myself, Mrs. Hunter, and put a stop to this shameful proceeding."

"God wull bless ye fur it, mem," said the widow fervently, "an' noo A'll no keep ye back by talkin' till ye, as ye hae jest little eneuch time. Guid-bye tae ye fur the praisent."

"Good-bye, Mrs. Hunter; you can find your way out, I suppose"; and with these parting words she flew off to dress and start upon her mission.

She arrived, as my readers are aware, too late. Had she been a few minutes earlier upon the scene the melancholy death of Corney might not have occurred. As she entered the wretched hovel the men took off their hats, and in respectful silence formed a passage for her to approach where Corney lay. Annie Brown took in all at a glance.

"Is he dead!" she asked in alarm.

"Yes, miss, *murdered!*" said the schoolmaster, solemnly.

Annie turned towards Taylor, and despite her agitation did not fail to note that there was a tear in his eye, and a look of profound sorrow, mingled with indignation, upon his face.

"*Murdered!*" she inquired.

"Yes, Miss Brown, murdered; it is true he could not have lived very much longer, but Ben's cruel act snapped the thread of life. There are witnesses here to corroborate my words."

"Ay, mem, it's ower true what the mester says," said several.

"Poor old Corney," murmured the girl, covering her face with her handkerchief and sobbing audibly. Touched by the sight, many a stout, broad-shouldered son of the sod drew his sleeve across his eyes, and several of them quietly slipped out to the open air.

For several minutes she stood thus, then turning to Taylor she enquired in a quivering voice how it had all happened.

Thus appealed to, Taylor, in a few sentences, told her all.

"My father knew nothing of this," said Annie, when Taylor had finished; "I know it was his wish that the old man should be kept comfortable till the end of his life. Poor old Corney! Mr. Taylor, I shall regard it as a personal favour if you will see to his decent interment. My father will pay all expenses."

Then casting another look upon the dead body, she gently inclined her head towards Taylor, drew her veil over her face and glided from the hut.

CHAPTER XI

HOW THE NEWS SPREAD

THE schoolmaster informed his farmer friends of what had passed between him and the squire's daughter, and a brief consultation was held.

"We have been talkin' ower amang us here what ye said aboot Corney bein' murdered," said Tom Gaw; "dae ye no think, mester, that Ben cud be punished for what he did? There's nae doot he killed the puir buddy."

Before Taylor could reply, another farmer, named M'Cutcheon, interfered, saying—

"Tak' care that some o' oorsels michtnae get intil trubble as weel as Black Ben."

"What fur?" asked Sam Stewart.

"Fur meddlin' wi' the business ava," replied M'Cutcheon.

"No muckle fear o' that," said a man named Keating; "everything o' the soart shud be put a stap tae. If ivery buddy wud treat these bailiff buddys the wae Jack M'Kay, o' Bellyhey, did, fowk wudnae be bothered wi' them."

"What wus that?" enquired a man who lived at a distance from the locality.

"Why," said Keating, "Jack had a very wild bull. The bailiffs went intae his byre yin day tae mak a saizure, and they took a' his kye, but left the bull ahint them. 'Why dint ye tak them a'? sez Jack. 'Oh, we hae here what'll dae us,' sez the bailiffs. 'Deed,' sez Jack,'if ye tak yin ye'll tak a', an' wi' that he turned oot the bull. Weel there wuz fun then. The bull made a teer at yin o' the bailiffs frae Newtown and sent him very near the heicht o' the hoose. The tithers tuk till their heels for it, and in less nor an hooer the hale cuntry wuz up aboot Jack's hoose."

HOW THE NEWS SPREAD

"It's as true as the gospel," said Tom Gaw, "an' there was nae mair aboot it; but apart frae that A want tae hear what the mester thinks aboot this affair o' Corney's."

"I am convinced," replied Taylor, "that Ben's act hastened the dissolution; but I am equally certain that nothing would result from any effort of ours to have the brute punished."

"Heth an' A wud speek till Major Mathews or Squire Leslie aboot it," said another farmer.

"Do as you please," said Taylor; "but for my part I am opposed to that course; I have faith in the justice of an overruling Power, and we may all live to see Black Ben meeting with his deserts. Leave him to Providence and his own conscience."

"Conscience!" growled one of the farmers, "Ben niver had yin."

"Well now, friends," said Taylor, "the first thing to be done is to get the old man decently buried. I had thought of increasing the money I gave him last night to whatever sum would be required for his interment, but Miss Brown has said that her father will do that. Poor old Corney! I little thought when selling tickets for the 'Punch Ball' that he would not need the money. Well, friends, I can promise that Mrs. Hunter will attend to the proper clothing of the dead. What about the coffin?"

There was a pause, and then Hugh M'Cutcheon spoke—

"Am gaun ower wi' a pickle corn tae Magilton's mill this efternoon," said he, "an' A wud think it nae bother tae call wi' John Byers, o' Bellyvester, an' order it there."

"Ye cudnae gang till a dacenter man," remarked another.

"'Tis a long distance to send," said Taylor.

"Weel it is," said M'Cutcheon, "but it's no' sae far oot o' my road, an' he'll hae sum chance o' sendin' it here on a cart the morrow."

"Whaur wull ye bury him?" asked Sam Stewart, who up till now had not spoken.

"I can tell you that," replied Taylor. "His wife, of whom, I am told, he was very fond, sleeps in the old graveyard of Templepatrick, and he has often told me it was his wish to lie there. Her grave is close to the old watchhouse."

"He'll hae mair fowk at his funeral nor them that haes dee'd worth plenty o' money," remarked a neighbour.

"Ay, ye may say that," said another, "an' A'm mistaen if his daith diznae cause a stir yit in the country."

"*It will!*" said Sam Stewart. And Sam was right.

The tidings of Corney O'Neill's death spread over the Ards like wild-fire. It is astonishing how rapidly news travels in rural districts where there are neither telephonic nor telegraphic stations. Many a bitter malediction was hurled at the head of Ben the bailiff, and that wretch, had he shown himself out of doors, would have met with handling the reverse of tender.

When Taylor left Corney's hut he went straight to Mrs. Hunter's cottage, but that worthy woman had heard the sad news before he arrived. She had returned from the squire's, had put aside her Sunday gear, and was in the act of boiling a pot of potatoes for dinner, when Jensie Duncan, a half-witted woman, who travelled the country for miles around, entered her cottage.

"Guid hae mercy on us, Mistress Hunter!" she exclaimed, "hae ye heerd the news?"

Mrs. Hunter started.

"What news, Jensie?" she asked.

"He's deid! he's kilt! he's murdered!" said Jensie in a loud voice.

Widow Hunter turned pale, and for a moment seemed dazed. A sudden fear seized upon her and seemed to stop the pulsations of her heart, as she gasped—"Wha's murdered, Jensie!"

"Corney O'Neill," said Jensie.

Widow Hunter sat down and pressed her hands upon her

HOW THE NEWS SPREAD

breast. For a moment her eyes went upwards as if she were wafting her silent thanks to heaven that her fears had not been realised. Then she questioned Jensie, who glibly related all she had heard and far more. She distorted the facts without compunction and told a tale of horror sufficient to awe a stouter heart than that of her hearer.

Jensie having received a slice of bread, thickly buttered, and a few pence, hurried off to repeat her story to the wondering people whom she met or at whose houses she called.

Ere Jensie had left Widow Hunter's, the schoolmaster entered, and from his lips the good widow heard the plain unvarnished tale. Her sympathetic nature was deeply touched by the recital, and she wept bitterly. When she regained her composure Taylor told her the nature of his errand.

"I have come," he said, "to ask you to dress, or assist in dressing Old Corney. I have written out an order for the necessary articles. I met Robert Wallace coming from the Squire's and he kindly volunteered to deliver my letter and to have the parcel forwarded to you by Brown's breadcart, which comes this way early to-morrow."

"A wull dae that, mester; A wull indeed," replied the widow; "Mary Fisher is richt an' handy wi' her needle, and A'll get her tae help me."

"And now, I must be off to my school," said Taylor; "I should not have been so long absent; good-bye, Mrs. Hunter, I'll be over to-night at Corney's wake."

Our readers will kindly accompany us to the wake.

CHAPTER XII

CORNEY'S WAKE

FROM time immemorial it has been the custom—amongst Sons of the Sod at all events—to "wake" the dead. The ancient custom may or may not be a good one, yet it is likely to prevail for a long time to come. I do not urge anything against the practice save this—that the proceedings are not at all times in keeping with the solemnity of the occasion. Too frequently an amount of levity prevails which must be painful to all sensitive minds, and especially to the bereaved relatives, who would naturally prefer not to be favoured with the presence of their well-meaning but thoughtless neighbours.

As a matter of course there was a "wake" at the hut of Corney O'Neill. Kindly hands had washed the body of the poor old man, and spread over it a snow-white sheet. Seats in abundance were provided from neighbouring houses; a large turf fire blazed on the hearth; numerous candles were lighted; there was a table well stocked with oatcake, cheese, tumblers and jugs, and but for the ghastly outline of that *something* stretched in the corner, one would have said that a harvest home was the business on hands. One by one the people dropped in until the place was crowded to inconvenience. The women had all retired after having made such arrangements as they could for the comfort of the sitters. It was surprising what a long distance some of the people had come. A reference has already been made to Harry O'Neill, old Corney's only son. Harry had been a good lad; kind-hearted, but restless and mischievous. He had been at every school in the district within a radius of four or five miles; now taking a turn at one and now at another, according to his humour; and though his tricks would, if played by most other boys, have led to expulsion, somehow Harry always escaped with a rebuke or a few cuts of the cane. He was a great favourite with all the schoolmasters, and now that his father was dead, and Harry, no one knew where, many of the Ards teachers came to spend an hour at the wake. Old Dominie Harvey, from Ballyboley, was there; James Kane, the teacher of Ballyvester National School, was there; and, amongst others, Andrew Wright, then in charge of the Herdstown school, near Donaghadee.

It is needless to say that the company included young Taylor and Johnnie Hunter. There were also present—David Henry, of Carrowdore; John Carelton, of Kirkantoon (Kirkistown); Whulty Regan, the tailor; Tam Dowlin, the Greyabbey postmaster; young Teugh (tough) M'Kay; Sam M'Givern; Davey Askin, the cow-doctor; Robin Byers; John Muckleboy; Wully Yeaman; Andy Hamilton; Alick Dorrian; Pat Brennan; Jamey Eccles; Johnnie Conway; John Gibson (the story-teller); Billy Magee; Wully Waddel, of Greyabbey; Alick Murphy; Gummery Patton; John M'Cluskey; and Sammy Reid, who prescribed for cancer, of which disease he professed to know five-and-twenty kinds. Last, but not least, amongst those to be mentioned, was Sammy Collins, a most eccentric Son of the Sod. Sammy was a merchant on a small scale. In those days, as at present, the value of old horses for the manufacture of manure, was fully appreciated. Sammy bought up all antediluvian specimens of the horse tribe and sold them to the knacker; he was also the possessor of a conveyance, of the cart species, in which he vended turf and bog fir from Donaghadee to Portaferry. He could be recognised at a long distance by his "Heelan bonnet," which was almost as well known then as is Harry Creevy's[*] in the present day, and he was always called "The Truncher" by the people of the district.

---

[*] Harry Creevy was a well-known hermit-eccentric from Greyabbey.

And now, having briefly introduced to my readers the principal inmates of Corney's hut, let us proceed to give an outline of the proceedings at the wake. The conversation was, for a long time, dull and carried on in subdued tones. Touching allusions were made to Corney and the many kind acts which had endeared him to his neighbours. The funeral arrangements were talked over; the hour for interment fixed, and a dozen men told off to "warn" the people in their various districts of the time at which the funeral cortege would start. Then a portion of scripture was read by an elder from the neighbouring church, and prayer was offered up by Mr. David Henry. After that a number left and the proceedings assumed a different form. Dominie Harvey, who regarded himself as somewhat of a leader upon such occasions, rose to his feet, and as he did so there was a hush in the murmur of conversation. The Dominie, as he was called, merits a brief passing notice. He was not far removed from the type of the hedge schoolmaster; but, in his own opinion he was a person of some importance. School fees in those days were pitifully small, but the Dominie's expenses were not large. His pupils carried him turf under their arms, so he had no fuel to purchase. Their parents supplied him with food, and he did not hesitate to billet himself upon their homes. "John Thompson," he would say to one pupil, stroking him on the head, "tell your ma I'll be over for dinner to-day; and Sam Bailey," stepping over to another "tell your father I'll look round to-night for a cup of tea." And thus the good Dominie subsisted and was happy. He was somewhat strict with his pupils and enjoined cleanliness as being next in importance to the payment of school fees and bi-weekly delivery of turf. If the Dominie noticed a boy entering the schoolroom with a face not over clean, it was usual for him to stamp his foot upon the floor and exclaim—

"You dirty little fellow! Where did you wash your face this morning? Was it in the parritch pot or in the pig's trough?"

The Dominie was a gossip. He collected all the news of the country and vended it industriously, adding a little bit here and there just to spice the dainty morsels. This trait in the worthy schoolmaster's character made him none the less welcome in his visits through the district. Indeed his visits were always welcome, and when one neighbour, in detailing the latest bit of scandal to another, said, "It's as true as the Gospel, for A hae it frae Dominie Harvey," the matter was at once beyond dispute. The Dominie's devices for acquiring local news were various and clever. He would, in the present day, have been an invaluable correspondent for a country newspaper. At the time of which I write, postal arrangements had not attained their present perfection. Tam Dowlin carried the letters from Greyabbey to Ballywalter, while through the district of which I am at present writing, they were delivered by a woman who bore the somewhat singular nickname (to use the local word) of "Crackenfudge." Both these worthies passed the door of Dominie Harvey, and neither of them ever passed without having a word with the schoolmaster. The Dominie knew the weak points of both and used them for his own purposes. Dowlin was a bachelor, and his weakness was to fall in love with nearly every woman he saw. Crackenfudge was but poorly educated and had hard work in deciphering the addresses upon her letters.

"Good morning, Tom," the Dominie would say, smilingly, as he observed Tam Dowlin approaching him. "Ah, Tom! you're a dreadful man with the ladies. Another heart broken at the soiree last week."

"An' wha micht that be, Dominie?" Tam would eagerly enquire.

"Ah, now, Tom, you don't know, I'm sure! But I dare not tell you, my man; I must not even give you the first letters of her name; that would be a breach of confidence you know. Let me see now; likely you have a letter for her this morning, let me see now."

Then Tom, gushing over with anxiety to hear of his new conquest, would slyly disclose to the Dominie the contents of his bag. But the Dominie was a cunning old fellow and generally had the best of it. Then came Crackenfudge, her face wrinkled with her attempts to read the superscription of her missives, and glad was she to be hailed by the Dominie. "Dear, dear!" she would exclaim; "A dae wush ye wud lern the fowk tae write plain. A'm shair they canna read these themsels. A suppose they take me tae be a better skolard nor they ir."

"Yes, no doubt great ignorance prevails"; the Dominie would answer. "A lady showed me an account yesterday from a neighbouring grocer that you know well. That account was for the small amount of four shillings, and yet it read £400."

"Bliss me, Dominie! Hoo was that?"

"Ignorance, my dear woman; ignorance. The man put the figures '4, 0, 0,' all in the space meant for pounds sterling, and when his mistake was pointed out to him, he just laughed and replied, 'Agh! what the divil aboot a wheen o' noughts.'"

And while the Dominie talked he deciphered for the woman the address which puzzled her and also mentally noted ALL that she carried in her hands.

The Dominie also conducted family worship at numerous houses which he visited, and the following perfectly true story is worth recording. One day he was thus engaged in prayer, the members of the household kneeling around him, when he was startled by a slight noise, and opened his eyes. A cat had leaped upon a table and was approaching a bowl of new milk. "Piss cat!" said the Dominie in a low voice. Pussy retired a short distance and prayer was resumed. But the Dominie had his eyes upon the animal, and as it again approached the vessel, he repeated his warning, "Piss cat!" in a louder tone. Pussy, however, grew bold; and popping her head into the bowl, began to lap up the delicious fluid. This was more than Dominie Harvey could stand, so, picking up a turf, he flung it at the thief, which instantly bolted. Then the Dominie, smiling upon his tittering companions, quietly remarked—"That's better than twenty 'piss cats!'"

But I have more than sufficiently diverged. I have said that Dominie rose to speak. His words, as reported by one who was present, were to the following effect:—

"Men and brethren, we have met upon a solemn occasion, and we are in the presence of death. An old residenter has just gone to that bourne from whence no traveller returns, and it is to show our respect for him that we are here. There will be a talk about this affair for many a long day to come, and there's one man in whose shoes I would not wish this night to stand. I need not mention his name, but the first letters of it are BLACK BEN. (This was a habit of the Dominie's.) However, my friends, it is not good at all times to mourn. We are told in the Book to give strong drink to those who are faint. Now grief maketh man faint and weary, and we all being in grief to-night are of necessity faint and weary, and that being so, it is our duty to have something to drink. That, my friends, is as clear as the simplest problem which I could propound to you in mathematics. Now, we have here a plentiful supply of good bread and cheese, and Sam M'Givern has just arrived with a couple of gallons of whiskey, so I propose that some of the younger men should now proceed to spill it out in order that our hearts may rejoice and be glad."

A murmur of suppressed approval followed the words of the Dominie, and at once Sam M'Givern, Andy Hamilton, Johnnie Hunter, and others set to work. The jar was uncorked and the liquor emptied into jugs. Some had punch, others grog, and all partook of bread and cheese. The effect of the spirit was marvellous. The presence of death was forgotten; the weather and farming operations were discussed; the rent question debated; Black Ben denounced; the news of the country discussed; every item of gossip talked over; births, deaths, and marriages, past and prospective; the price of farm produce; the clergy, the doctors, the lawyers, the grocers, the publicans—these and countless other subjects kept every tongue wagging as glass after glass of the potent liquor was swallowed. At last the Dominie was asked to tell a story. Nothing could more have pleased the Dominie, and he rattled off a score of them in quick succession.

"Gentlemen," he said, "I meet with some amusing incidents in the course of my scholastic life and duties. In Greyabbey the other day a woman, whose name I needn't mention, was getting upon a car to go to Newtownards. The driver could not prevail upon her to sit upon the cushions. Placing herself upon the footboard she said, quite firmly, 'A'll dae heer richtly; A'm nae wae prood, an' A'll lee the cushions fur the genteels.'"

There was a laugh at this, and several cried out—

"It's jest the truth, Dominie; A ken richt weel wha she wuz."

"The Rev. Mr. Jeffrey," resumed the Dominie, "was visiting at a house where I myself was to have dinner the other day, and the mistress of the house very kindly asked his reverence to join us in our meal. Now this good woman is by no means liberal in payment of stipend and always pleads poverty. On this particular occasion there was a fine plump hen boiled for dinner, and as the woman helped Mr. Jeffrey to a leg of the fowl, she said, 'A hope yer reverence'll no think me extravagant in hevin' a hen fur denner. It's a thing we niver taste here, *but this yin tuk the trakes,** *an' A thocht A wud jest cut the heid aff her.*'"

"Weel din, Dominie; fill up yer glass an' tell us another," said Alick Dorrian, amid a roar of laughter.

---

* i.e., got sick, took diarrhoea.

"I will do that," replied the worthy. "Talking of the hen reminds me of an incident which occurred in Newtownards. A pig became somewhat sickly and refused its food. The mistress returning to the kitchen one day with a bucket of its untasted food, remarked to her son John, in a petulant tone of voice, that she wished the pig was dead. Now this son John is somewhat of a wag, so quietly lifting a hatchet he slipped out, got astride the pig's back and split its skull. Returning to the house, he put the hatchet in its place and turning to his mother coolly remarked—*The pig's deid noo.*'"

There was another laugh as the Dominie drained his glass, smacked his lips, and prepared for a further effort.

"I had my breakfast in Ballymurphy the other morning," he said. "The good woman who entertained me is very shortsighted. She took a piggin of milk and offered it to what she thought was the calf, but which was, in reality, a lump of bog fir. Of course the milk was not accepted. 'Tak' it up ye thing!' said the woman giving the piggin a shake. Still no sign of acceptance. 'Tak' it up, A say, an' no keep me stannin' here a' day!' cried the woman, growing angry. Then fairly losing patience, she dashed the milk over the fir block, exclaiming, 'There, noo, *if it's no in ye it's on ye.*'"

Thus did the old fellow rattle away.

"Why dae ye no get married?" asked Sam M'Givern.

"I'll tell you that," answered the Dominie; "I was never a good hand at courting. I am something like a Ballyboley man, of whom you have probably heard, who was very timid. On one occasion when going to court he filled his pockets with cold potatoes for the dog, and on coming back he tripped in a field, and fell over Abram Brown's horse. 'That'll dae me for coortin'!' muttered the man, as he gathered himself up."

This last story appeared to tickle the company immensely, and sundry nods and winks were directed towards Sam himself.

By this time some of the stewards seemed oblivious to their duties; and so, Sam M'Givern stepped nimbly about, helping such as were yet too shy to help themselves, and all the while giving vent to his favourite exclamations—"Hide-an-hare!" "Life in London!" "Teer me up!" "Corn in Egypt!" "Matty White, Jean Tate an' Wailly Wuds!"

What Sam meant by these singular phrases I cannot tell; probably, if yet living, he could not tell himself.

"Noo, A think Teugh M'Kay micht tell us a story," said Whulty Regan.

"Oh, let Teugh alane!" said Tam Dowlin "he's that busy coortin' Bel Herron that he haesnae even time in the mornin's tae luk oot on Colville's Hill for the French Turkey."

There was a roar of laughter at that, but Teugh M'Kay was not in the least disturbed. He merely removed the blackened clay pipe from his mouth and expectorated, noisily and copiously.

"Teugh haes a guid wheen o' them on hands," remarked Sam M'Givern. "Teer me up! but he'll no let the name dee oot any wae. Life in London! what'll his aunty say if he taks Bel Herron hame?"

"A hope A'll get the order for the waddin' suit," said Whulty.

"Nae sich thing," said Sam Wright, "ye may be shair he'll gie the order tae nane but Alick Murphy, o' Cardy. Ye ken he maks for the Squires an' gran' fowk."

M'Kay laughed, and lifting a farl of oat cake and a huge lump of cheese, attacked them as though he had not tasted food for a week.

"Luk at him!" exclaimed M'Givern; "coortin' diznae tak' awa his appetite. Hide-an-hare! he can tak' bites oot o' a bannock like the fleers o' a hake!"*

---

* 'fleers o' a hake!': the meaning here is uncertain, but presumably refers to the fearsomely sharp, curved teeth of the hake fish and its

CORNEY'S WAKE

"He's no' like John Carleton," said Whulty. "John was that bad in love that he went tae bed yin nicht wi' a' his claes on. A dinnae ken whuther he got ony sleep or no, but whun his ma went in the next mornin' he had kickit the taes oot o' his shoon an' et the hale en' oot o' the bowster!"

But my readers may be weary of the wake, so I shall shift the scene.

---

projecting lower jaw. A 'fleer' can be defined as a 'grin' or 'grimace'.

CHAPTER XIII

CORNEY'S FUNERAL

IT was daylight when Dominie Harvey and his jolly companions left Corney's hut, to return again for a second night, which was spent in a manner somewhat similar to that described in the preceding chapter. The Dominie, having given his pupils a holiday, he was not under the necessity of returning to Ballyboley until after the funeral, and he therefore ensconced himself in Widow Hunter's armchair, where he spent the day in his accustomed fashion, that is to say, in eating, drinking, telling stories, and enjoying an occasional nap.

After dinner hour—the Sons of the Sod dine early—those who had been told off to "warn" the neighbours of the time fixed for the funeral, started off upon their errand, and, ere night closed in, the people had been warned for miles around. Poor Corney's last outfit arrived in due time, and was tenderly placed upon the dead; the coffin came from John Byers, and Corney's mortal remains were enclosed therein. There was no hearse. The roads were bad, and, although the distance to be traversed was a long one, Corney must be borne upon the shoulders of his old acquaintances. This they would willingly have done, even had the journey been double the length. In those days only the wealthy procured hearses.

And now, as noon approached, the people were observed coming from every direction. Some travelled by the highways, others crossed the fields. They came from Greyabbey, from Cardy, from Ballyboley, from Carrowdore, from Donaghadee, from Millisle and from the neighbouring townlands. The funeral was one of the largest ever seen in the district. When the procession approached the place of interment it was joined by

CORNEY'S FUNERAL

several gentlemen who had known Corney as a faithful servant of Squire Brown, and who put in an appearance chiefly from a feeling of respect for the latter. Amongst these were the Rev. David Parke, the esteemed pastor of Carrowdore Presbyterian congregation, and father of the late Dr. R. C. Parke, J.P., then a lad of promise, a general favourite, and later the popular Coroner for North Down; the Rev. David Jeffrey, of Greyabbey—who came in his gig; the Rev. John Macauley, of Ballyvester; Dr. Shaw, of Greyabbey; and Dr. Catherwood, of Donaghadee. As some of these gentlemen are to figure somewhat prominently in this story, I content myself by merely referring to them here.

The locality of Templepatrick graveyard and its appearance are so familiar to the people of the Ards that little need be said of it. It lies upon the margin of the sea, about a mile and a quarter from Donaghadee, on the Millisle road which forms one of its boundaries. The graveyard is much the same now as it was then; a small plot of ground hemmed in by the sea on one side and by the county road on another, covered with long grass and tangled weeds that grow luxuriantly, while in its centre stand the walls of a watch-house erected in the days of body snatching, and within which the people took their turn night after night to guard the bodies of the dead from desecration. The surroundings have considerably changed. The beautiful edifice erected by Mr. William Carmichael looks down from its gracefully sloping and shrub-crowned eminence upon the old graveyard; a tall pole marks alike the position of the submarine telegraph cable and the onward march of scientific discovery. The old homestead of Mr. Hugh M'Kee, Mr. Thomas Brown, and other well-known farmers, nestle near to the spot, looking none the worse of thirty years' exposure to the elements.

It is needless to say that the people could not find accommodation on the burying-ground. Indeed the place was taken up by parties from Millisle and the neighbourhood long before the funeral cortege had arrived. They, therefore, lined the roadway, and stood upon the beach and other places. As already stated, Corney's deceased wife had been interred beside the watch-house, and the old man had expressed a wish to lie in the same grave. Mr. Thomas Brown, of Millerhill, and Mr. Hugh M'Kee had each sent a man to open the grave, and now all was in readiness to commit "Dust to dust." When the coffin had been lowered to its final resting place every head was uncovered, and the deathly stillness was unbroken save by the sullen murmur and splash of the waves as they broke upon the sandy beach or dashed upon the rugged rocks that bound the Kinnegar. A portion of Scripture was read by the Rev. David Jeffrey, and a brief address delivered by the Rev. David Parke. The latter gentleman died many years ago, after a long, useful, and well-spent life. His ashes now repose in the sandy soil of Ballycopeland graveyard, which lies within a short distance of the scene of Corney's burial. Mr. Parke was dearly beloved by his people, and many there are who till this day remember his words at Corney's grave. He referred to the loyalty manifested by Corney to his employer; to the regularity of his attendance, while in health, at the House of God; to the respect shown to him by the vast crowd of people now standing around the humble grave of a humble man. "And now, dear friends," he continued, "you will naturally expect some allusions from me to the mode of his death. This is a subject with which I will do well to deal briefly, lest I should stir up in your minds feelings which are in antagonism to Christianity. Poor Corney was, as most of you know, completely worn out. His sands of life had run. Indeed, the wonder is that he had lived so long. It is to be regretted that he was disturbed in the last hour of his long life; that even as the Angel of Death swooped down to summon the spirit of the old man from its frail tenement of clay, the hands of a bailiff should be laid upon Corney to thrust his body, weak and worn as it was, from the wretched and tottering walls which afforded him but a miserable shelter from the wintry blast. I grant you, my friends, that the conduct of the man to whom I refer was cruel and unjust, but let not angry passions swell in your hearts against him. Corney has gone; in this narrow grave lies all that is mortal of him. I believe his spirit has gone to a bright world—to a place where there are no evictions. God has snatched him from the hands of those who would have shown him little mercy, and to that God let us leave his avenging, if avenging there should be. 'Vengeance is Mine, I will repay,' saith the Lord. Bear this in recollection; return peaceably and quietly to your homes, and do not attempt to violate the laws either of God or of your country. Some day I, too, shall be laid in my grave; so shall you all. Let us, then, lead blameless lives, so that when we are called away there may be none to speak ill of us. Let us pray."

The Rev. John Macaulay offered up an affecting prayer; the clay was shovelled in upon the coffin, and, as the people departed for their respective homes, many a coat sleeve and many a cotton handkerchief was raised to wipe away the falling tear.

CHAPTER XIV

SQUIRE BROWN

A WEEK had elapsed since Corney was buried. A meeting of farmers had been held in Taylor's schoolhouse, at which a deputation had been appointed to wait upon Squire Brown with a view to bring under his notice the dastardly conduct of Black Ben, and also his general mode of dealing with the tenants. It was the wish of the meeting that the young schoolmaster should accompany them, but Taylor disapproved of this, and pointed out his reasons for doing so. He promised, however, to give all the help in his power, and drew up a letter to be addressed to the Squire on the subject.

It was a fine, bright, frosty morning. The sparrows twittered upon Squire Brown's thatch and among his stacks of grain; the blackbirds hopped about the bit of lawn; the noisy inhabitants of the fowlyard kept up an incessant clamour. It was breakfast hour, and the Squire, with his daughter, sat at table in the parlour, with its cosy but old-fashioned furniture. The Squire was a gloomy, morose man, and of little speech. He preferred to sit alone, save at meal times. Now and then he would chat freely, almost cheerily, with his pretty daughter, but at other times the meal was eaten in silence. On the present occasion the Squire was in rather an amiable mood. Happening to look in the direction of the front window he observed a woman entering the gate.

"Annie," he said, "there's Crackenfudge; you might see what letters she has."

"Yes, papa," said Annie, hurrying to open the door, for she expected some letters herself. She was not disappointed; so, placing her own missives upon the hall table, she returned to the breakfast parlour with her father's. One of them was large; it looked like a sheet of foolscap awkwardly folded, and fastened with paste or starch. Having deposited the Squire's letters before him, she hastened to the kitchen, whither she had sent Crackenfudge for breakfast. Annie directed Jane, the servant, to see the letter carrier make a hearty breakfast, whereupon that worthy wheeled round from the fire at which she was thawing her half-frozen fingers, and thus addressed her—

"Ay, mem; you hae some sense wi' ye; there's a wheen o' wud-be quelity through the country an' they're naethin' but dirt so they ir. A left a letter at a certain hoose this mornin' an' the mistress sent me a pancake tae the daur. A sent it back till her, an' sez I, jes tell her A dinnae carry letters fur pancakes!"

"Well, now; see that you take a good breakfast," said Annie, as she darted off to her own room to peruse her letters. There were three. The addresses of two were in a familiar hand. That of the third she did not recognise. This one she opened first. It bore neither date nor address, but the following words were written in a clear, bold hand:—

> *Miss Brown, your father is a stranger to his tenantry, and Black Ben oppresses them. They love you and you can help them. Intercede with your father upon their behalf. Have Ben sent about his business or Corney O'Neill's death may be avenged.*
>
> A FRIEND."

A strange feeling crept into Annie's heart as she read this. Who could the writer be? How should she act? Before she could give these questions further consideration there was a tap at the door.

"Come in," said Annie, slipping the letter into her bosom.

Jane, the servant, popped in her head, looking flurried.

"Master wants you, Miss," she said; "something has vexed him. Please come quick!"

Annie flew down stairs to her father's room. She found him pacing about the apartment, and evidently in a towering passion.

"What's the matter, papa?" she enquired anxiously.

"Read that!" he said, handing her the bulky letter already referred to.

It was a request, civilly worded, and signed by nearly a dozen of his tenants, asking him to name an hour for receiving them upon a matter of importance to him and them.

"Well, papa, won't you see them?" she ventured to ask.

"What the devil do they want?" he growled. "Reduction of rent, I suppose. Let them talk to Ben. I can't be troubled with them."

"But it may not be that," said Annie; "in fact, papa, I have an idea that I know what this means."

"How can you know, child?" he asked.

"I do not say that I actually know," she answered, "but something tells me that this has a reference to Ben himself." And her mind reverted to the anonymous communication which lay in her breast.

"Ah, very likely!" muttered the Squire; "ugly business that of Corney O'Neill's. Ben's a useful fellow, but he's a brute. I've not yet spoken to him about that affair. Annie, send Jane round to say that I want him instantly."

"Yes, papa," said Annie, and she hurried away, glad to leave him in his present humour. The next minute Jane had gone to Ben's quarters to deliver the Squire's message. She paused for a moment, with her hand upon the latch, for Ben's dog had sprung against the door, uttering a savage growl.

CHAPTER XV

LANDLORD AND BAILIFF

BLACK BEN ordered the dog to lie down, and the brute—ugly and surly as its master—obeyed the command. Then Ben opened the door and Jane stepped in. She did so, however, with an evident air of caution, looking from side to side of the kitchen as she came slowly forward.

"Ir ye feered o' ocht?" asked the bailiff, in a half-angry, half-bantering tone.

"Weel, A think A em, Ben"; Jane replied; "A dae not ken what ye keep sich a beest o' a dug aboot the hoose fur."

"Tae keep aff the theeves," said Ben.

"There's nae theeves hereaboots, Ben," said Jane; and then she added with a saucy toss of her head—"Yer ugly enough lukin' tae scaur the very auld Nick yersel', so ye ir."

"Yer aye tellin' me that, Jane, but ye cud fin' waur fowk nor me," remarked Ben.

"A dinnae ken whaur it would be," said Jane; "but A'm forgettin' my errand; the Squire wants ye at the big hoose this very minit."

A look of uneasiness came upon Ben's face. He had been hourly expecting this summons; he knew for what purpose he was wanted, and he dreaded the interview.

"A'll be efter ye in a minute," he said; and Jane departed at a run.

Ben stood for some minutes looking into the fire. His hands were plunged deep in his trousers pockets; his brows were knit, his face darker and uglier than ever.

"A ken what he wants wi' me," he muttered; "but A suppose the suiner its ower the better."

Saying this, he put on his hat and passed out, locking the door behind him.

A few minutes afterwards Ben stood face to face with the Squire. There was a wonderful change now in his appearance and manner, for Ben could suit himself to circumstances, and as he stood now, in respectful silence, hat in hand, few would have discovered the real character of the man.

"Well, Ben," said the Squire, "I have sent for you to get the whole particulars of that unfortunate affair at Corney O'Neill's. Sit down; be as brief as possible, but tell me all the facts."

"There's no muckle tae tell," said Ben, in a cringing voice, as he sat down upon a chair with his back to the window. "That auld den whaur Corney leev'd wuz a disgrace tae the country side, an' fur years back A cud a made a good lettin' o' it tae a man that wants tae bigg' a dacent hoose. There's dizens o' fowk wantid Corney tae gang an' leeve wi' them, but he was as thrawin' as a pig, and wudnae budge oot."

"Why didn't you consult with me?" said the Squire.

"Agh, A didnae want tae bother you," whined Ben; "A'm shair A did it fur the best; an' A wuz studying his interests as well as yours, Squire!"

"In what way, Ben?"

"Acause you would hae got an addition tae yer rents, an' sum o' the neibors wud a given Corney a comfortable home."

"I don't see it in that light by any means, Ben, and we may both have trouble about this matter. The people's talk has reached me, and they directly charge you with causing Corney's death."

"It's no true!" said Ben, "they a' hae a spite at me acause A luk efter their rents, an' A think A got the worst o' it, squire. That fellow Sam Stewart struck me a blow on the face that micht a kilt me. A'm shair A loast a quart o' bluid, an' my front teeth's a' lousened; A cannae bite a happorth ever since. A beleev in my heart it wuz Stewart frichtened Corney tae daith."

"That may all be, Ben," said the Squire; "but what I complain of is this; you acted in the affair without ever consulting me. Now the fact is, that I did not know even of Corney's existence; if I had, he would never have been in want, because I never had a more honest, trustworthy, hard-working fellow in my employment. As I said before, there may be trouble arising out of this. Several local magistrates have spoken to me and to my daughter about it, and this very hour I have a letter here asking me to receive a body of my tenants who wish to speak to me on a certain subject. Ben, I know what that subject is and so do you."

Ben twirled his hat nervously between his hands and sat silent. The Squire did not seem inclined to speak further, and so there was an awkward pause. At length Ben looked up, and enquired, somewhat eagerly—

"Wha ir they that wants tae see you?"

The Squire lifted the letter and adjusted his spectacles as though about to read the document to Ben, but after a moment he laid it down and said—

"That will do for the present, Ben. How do the rents stand?"

"There's a good wheen o' them ahint," replied Ben.

"Let me have a statement of them during the present week," said the Squire. "You may go now."

Ben left at once, glad to get away. The interview had passed off more quietly than he had anticipated. He repaired to his own quarters, and taking down the greasy, thumb-stained book which contained the entries of his rents, he proceeded to turn over its leaves in anything but an amiable mood. Now and then he muttered to himself, thinking audibly. "They'll be wantin' him tae sen' me aboot my business, A suppose. Weel, they hae the wrang soo by the lug this time, as sum o' them may fin' tae their coast!"

We shall leave Ben to pursue his labours and musings without further interruption.

CHAPTER XVI

LANDLORD AND TENANT

AT the period of which I write there was no Land Act. Farmers toiled then as they toil now; many of them—even in the prosperous Ards—dwelt in cheerless, uncomfortable houses; they lived upon the commonest fare; their children were uneducated; they rose early and worked late; they complained, and not without reason, of the rack-rents exacted by hard-hearted absentee landlords, and by brutal, purse-bound, overfed, ignorant agents and bailiffs; they prayed for a brighter day, for deliverance from their bondage, for the reward of their toil. "It is a long lane that has no ending." Could some prophetic soul have arisen to tell of Gladstone's great achievements—the Land Act and the Ballot Act—how the prophecy would have made many a heart leap for joy! There were many in those days who did not fear to denounce landlord tyranny. There were those who could see the edging of the silver lining to the cloud. The efforts of a Sharman-Crawford on behalf of the farmers of Ulster encouraged clergymen and others to speak out. Meetings were held over the country. Mr. Taylor, of Greyabbey, and many others whose names might be mentioned here, though then scarce out of their teens, were taking a lively interest in the question of Tenant-right.

I have said that, after the death of Corney O'Neill, a meeting of tenant farmers was held upon the property of Squire Brown. This, however, was of small moment compared with other gatherings, one of the largest and most influential of which was held in Greyabbey. This demonstration took the form of a tenant-right soiree. The demand for tickets was enormous. Two meeting-houses—the Rev. William Hall's and the Rev.

LANDLORD AND TENANT

David Jeffrey's—were required to accommodate the sitters. After tea all adjourned to the church of Mr. Hall—then a building of large dimensions. The meeting was one which had a marked effect upon neighbouring landlords, and it was one the recollections of which must be fresh in the minds of many who peruse these pages. The vast audience was deeply stirred by the addresses delivered, and at times the enthusiasm rose to a remarkable pitch. Amongst the assembly were many who have gone to rest and many who yet live to see and enjoy the fruits of the seed then being sown.

Mr. M'Knight, of the *Northern Whig*, the Rev. William Hall, the Rev. David Jeffrey, the Rev. David Parke, Mr. William Byers, and others were amongst the speakers. Conspicuous amongst the audience was Pat Hunter, landsteward for Mr. Montgomery. There were also present Dr. Shaw, William M'Kee, of Tullycavey; John Semple, John Johnston, Ballyhaft; Robert Byers, Ballyboley; Hugh Wright; Joseph Brown; William Little; R. O. Young; Hugh Taylor; William Woods, Blackabbey; Hugh M'Kelvey, Glastry; John Purse; Hugh Lowry; John Muckle; Hugh Dornan; John Barnes; Alex. Dorrian; Andrew Lutton; William Shaw, Kirkcubbin, and scores of others whose names are well known in that district.

The speech of the evening was beyond doubt that which was delivered by the Rev. Mr. Hall. This gentleman, who was pastor of the Unitarian body in Greyabbey, was exceedingly popular, not only amongst his own congregation, but with the members of other bodies. Possessed of a highly cultured mind and matured judgment, a warm heart, a generous nature, and an eloquent and graceful delivery, he secured at once the riveted attention of his hearers. I have before me, and would fain reproduce, copious extracts from his powerful speech of that night, in which he made touching references to Corney O'Neill, to the condition of the tenant farmers, and to the plan of action which they should adopt. But though Mr. Hall's speech would be read at the present time with feelings of the deepest interest, I must hasten on to the relation of the startling events which followed fast upon Black Ben's dastardly attempt to evict old Corney O'Neill.

CHAPTER XVII

THE PRODIGAL'S RETURN

ON the day of Ben Hanlon's interview with Squire Brown an event occurred which caused no little excitement in the locality, and but for which this story would in all probability never have been penned.

It was market day in Newtownards. Young Johnnie Hunter had gone thither to dispose of a cart load of potatoes; and his mother, active as usual, was bustling about her house in the pursuit of her usual avocations. The barking of her dog attracted the widow's attention, and she stepped out in order to ascertain the cause. On looking up the old cart road, to which reference has already been made, she observed a stranger approaching—a young man, neatly attired, and who stepped along the road with a free, easy step, looking from side to side in his walk as though noting with interest the striking points of the surrounding scenery. He was quite near to Mrs. Hunter's cottage, and the good woman, fearing to be thought inquisitive, went inside, taking Towser with her. But though she did return indoors, the curiosity so characteristic of the neighbourhood induced her to peep through the window and watch the stranger's movements. To her surprise he stopped at her garden gate, withdrew the bolt which fastened it as familiarly as though he had been in the daily habit of performing that act, stepped quickly up the garden path and entered the open door. The widow turned to him expecting him to make enquiry for some place in the neighbourhood and little anticipating the surprise in store for her. With a frank smile the stranger stepped up to Mrs. Hunter, and, grasping both her hands in his, exclaimed:—

"My dear Mrs. Hunter, how are you?"

"Thank ye, sir, A'm bravely," she answered, gazing into his face in wonder and without attempting to withdraw her hands.

"You don't recognise me, I see," said the stranger. "Come now, Mrs. Hunter, who am I?"

"A declare, sir, A dae not ken," she answered; "there's somethin' aboot yer e'en an' yer forheid that A think A hae seen afore, but yer a stranger tae me."

"Well, I won't be that much longer," he exclaimed. "I'm Harry O'Neill—Corney's son."

The widow withdrew her hands now, but it was to fling her arms round her visitor with a cry of glad surprise, and to imprint upon his cheek a warm, motherly kiss. Then she held him at arms' length, looking at him from head to foot, while delight, admiration and astonishment were visible in her every feature. At last she found tongue—

"Harry O'Neill!" she cried; "can A believe my e'en? An' yer growen a big man, an' a perfect gentleman tae; sit doon dear; here, there's the erm-chair that mony a time A nursed ye in."

She led him to the seat by the hand, and when he was seated she put aside his hat and stroked his head as she had so often done in bygone years when Harry, a wild, playful lad, was the inseparable companion of her own son, Johnnie.

"Yes, Mrs. Hunter, I have grown, as you say, to be quite a man, while you seem very little changed; but I am all impatience to hear the news of the country. Where are my father and mother? I've been at the old house, but found it empty and in ruins, so I came right off to you. Where are they, Mrs. Hunter?"

The widow's face saddened, and a tear-drop formed in her eye as she answered—

"Baith awa, Harry; baith awa!"

"Away where?" he asked eagerly.

"They're in Heaven, A'm shair," she whispered.

"Good God!" groaned Harry, burying his face in his hands;

"dead and gone without seeing me! Oh, this is dreadful." He could say no more. For several minutes not another word was spoken. Harry's vigorous frame shook with suppressed sobbing, and big tears trickled from between his fingers, which were clasped over his eyes, and dropped upon the hearthstone. Mrs. Hunter, too, was deeply moved, and she did not venture for a time to intrude upon the mourner's grief. By and by she placed her hand upon Harry's head, and said, in soothing tones—

"Dinna fret, dear. It's a peety ye didnae cum hame suiner, but it cannae be helpit noo."

"Tell me all about it," said Harry; "when did they die? Tell me all."

And Mrs. Hunter, sitting down beside him, told him how his mother had pined after his departure and died comparatively young; how his father talked of him and longed for his return, then gave him up for dead. She told him of Corney's death and burial, but she did not even hint at his poverty or at the sad event which had hastened his dissolution. And then, her story finished, she asked in a half reproachful voice—

"What's the raison ye niver sent a scrape o' a pen, Harry?"

"Don't ask me now, Mrs. Hunter; I'll explain all by-and-by," said Harry. "Where's Johnnie? Dead, too, I suppose; everything seems wrong."

"Na, thank God, Johnnie's leevin' an' weel," she answered; "he's awa' at Newtown the noo."

"My poor mother! my poor father!" murmured Harry; "to think that I should return to make you happy, to see you end your days in peace and plenty, and now to find you both dead. O, my God, it is dreadful!"

"God's will maun be din, dear, an' ye shudnae murn at what He diz," said Mrs. Hunter.

"I know that, I know that; but it is so hard to bear; the human heart will rebel, you know Mrs. Hunter."

Then Harry rose to leave. Mrs. Hunter pressed him to stay. She knew that at the very first house he went to the story of his father's death would be told him, and she did not wish him to hear this until the first burst of grief had passed off. She felt that she ought to tell him herself; she could break it off gently, yet her heart would not allow her to mention it just yet, and so she did what she could to prevail upon him to await Johnnie's return. Harry yielded to her wishes, and by degrees he brightened up.

Mrs. Hunter prepared him a cup of tea, and pressed it upon him so kindly that he could not refuse to take it, and while he sipped it she told him some of the news of the district, breaking off in the midst of it with—

"Yer niver axin' aboot yer wee sweetheart, Annie Broon."

Harry smiled—the change of subject touched another chord.

"I have not forgotten my little playmate," he said. "Tell me about her, Mrs. Hunter; is she as beautiful as ever? She'll be quite a woman now."

"Ay, man, she's bonnier nor iver she was; an' as guid as she's bonnie. It'll no be lang till ye pye her a visit, A reckon."

"I hope to have that pleasure before long, Mrs. Hunter. Her memory has sustained me in many a danger and difficulty, but we'll have a chat upon that subject some other time. Hilloa! here's a visitor whose face I surely recognise."

It was Dominie Harvey.

As he entered, Harry O'Neill met him with extended hands. It was some moments before the worthy old schoolmaster could believe his eyes or ears; but, when he really became convinced that Harry O'Neill, his old pupil, stood before him, he seemed literally to go wild with joy.

"Ha, my boy!" he exclaimed, as for the twentieth time at least he shook hands with him, "I always said you'd be something; you were a wild lad, Harry, but you had the brains. Bless me!

THE PRODIGAL'S RETURN

you're a perfect gentleman. Where have you been, my boy?"

"At the goldfields, Dominie, and Dame Fortune has smiled upon your pupil. Prepare for great doings in this part now."

The Dominie's face suddenly grew sad.

"Harry, my lad," he said, "I wish you had come sooner. That was a sad end your poor father had."

The widow darted a look of warning at the Dominie, but that worthy did not observe it.

"Of course, you have told him of it, Mrs. Hunter," he continued.

"How? What?" said Harry; "explain your meaning, good Dominie."

The Dominie turned to the widow.

"Have not you told him?" he asked.

"Na, Dominie, A hadnae the heart tae speak o' it. But it's oot noo, an' he wud a heerd it onywae. Dominie, naebuddy cud tell him better nor yersel."

And the Dominie told the story, while Harry sat like one in a dream. He spoke not a word during the Dominie's rehearsal of the sad facts. At the conclusion of the narrative Harry rose, quite calmly and composedly, but there was a dangerous look in his dark eyes.

"Yer no gaun awa," said the widow; "won't ye stap till Johnnie cums in frae Newtown?"

"No, Mrs. Hunter; but I'll see you soon. I am going to have a word with Black Ben."

"Oh, dear, dinnae gang near him," pleaded the widow, taking hold of Harry's hand. But he gently put her aside and stepped out.

"Dominie, dear, there'll be murder!" cried the widow. "Gang efter him, an' stap him."

The Dominie did as he was asked; but, ere he had reached the old cart road, Harry's fleet limbs had borne him round the turning and out of sight.

CHAPTER XVIII

THE AVENGER

HARRY O'NEILL strode along the old cartroad at a rapid pace. He heeded not now the old familiar landscape; he noted not the landmarks of his boyhood days. His brows were knit, his lips compressed, his hands clenched. His young blood boiled in his veins, rage and hate swelled his heart, one desire alone possessed his soul, and that was to crush the life out of the vile reptile who had disturbed the last moments of the life of an old worn-out, defenceless man.

Harry was wonderfully well developed, sturdy and strong for his years. Since that day when he left his father's humble dwelling he had lived an eventful life. Those who pursue in our little island the monotonous career of farming, commercial or professional life know but little of the mighty universe upon the surface of which they are the veriest atoms. But to those who go down to the sea in ships; who explore the vast regions of other lands; who delve into the bowels of the earth in search of her buried treasures—is reserved the sublimity of creation, the realisation of the Omnipotence of a Creator. Harry O'Neill had lived more in ten years—because he had seen and endured more—than others whose existence had far exceeded the allotted span; hazardous toil, privation, and adventure had hardened his muscles and developed a brave lad into a strong, bold, fearless man; his ardent spirit, trained in nature's school, owned no master and cringed to no superior. His ideas of justice were formed in a land where vengeance follows swiftly upon deeds of wrong, and now he was the avenger hurrying with rapid strides to claim that to which he felt he was entitled—blood for blood, a life for a life!

THE AVENGER

Such was the man with whom Ben the bailiff was to deal and account for his heartless deed. Harry knew Ben's quarters well, and a few minutes brought him to the door. "Curse him!" he muttered, as he placed his hand upon the latch and found the door fastened. Raising his foot he delivered a kick which made the timbers quiver, frame and all, bringing a shower of whitewashed plaster upon his head and shoulders.

"Wha's there?"

It was the harsh, guttural voice of Ben from within, and was immediately followed by the fierce barking of his dog.

"Open the door and you'll see!" replied Harry, in a voice hoarse with passion.

There was a sound of footsteps within. It was the bailiff crossing the floor, but he did not open the door. He peeped from the window instead. There was a small porch at the entrance, and thus Ben could see Harry where he stood. He did not recognise him, however. How could he? He discovered, though, that the visit was not a friendly one; he could read that in the white face of the stranger, with his clenched teeth and angry eyes. Harry did not perceive Ben's hasty inspection of him from the window, and the bailiff withdrew lest he might be seen.

"Blast it!" he muttered; "wha can it be? A wush A hadnae spauk!"

"Let me in, or I'll burst open the door!" cried Harry.

"What ir ye, and what dae ye want?" inquired Ben.

"I want you, Ben; let me in and then I'll tell you who I am and why I want you!" was the reply.

"Awa aboot yer business," growled Ben; "ye can hae nae business wi' me; if yer no oot o' that in less nor half a minute A'll hunt the dug efter ye."

Harry did not reply. He turned partly round, placed his right shoulder against the door and pushed with all his strength. The door was fastened by a latch and stout wooden bar, but they were mere straws when pitted against the muscles of the young gold digger. They snapped like reeds, and the door, with a crash, flew open so suddenly that Harry, had he not seized the stout framework, must have fallen into the porch.

"Catch him, boy!" shouted Ben to his dog.

But Harry was too quick for the brute, and the kick which he administered sent it sprawling and yelping into a corner. Then it dashed out of doors and rushed across the fields. At the same instant Ben made a motion as though to pick up his stout cudgel, but a look from Harry restrained him. He cursed himself in his heart for not having had the stick in his possession when the intruder entered. But then, that entrance was so sudden and unexpected!

"Now, Ben Hanlon, look at me and I'll tell you who I am," said Harry, quite calmly, yet in a voice that quivered from suppressed rage. "Look at me, Ben," he repeated, as the bailiff endeavoured to meet his indignant gaze. "You asked me who I was and what my business; now I'll tell you. I'm Harry O'Neill, and I have come here to avenge the murder of my old father."

Every drop of blood fled from Ben's cheeks, and the hand which he had clenched as though about to strike the man who confronted him, fell by his side, as though suddenly deprived of power. There was silence for a moment, but only for a moment. Ben, struggling against the craven fear which was fast taking possession of his heart, recovered his presence of mind, and assuming a defiant air, said—

"A hae naethin' tae dae wi' that; A knowed ye cudnae hae ony business wi' me."

"Yes, but I *have* business with you, Ben, and you know it; I can read your knowledge from your face; you murdered my father, Corney O'Neill."

Ben uttered a sneering laugh. "Ye'd better min' what yer

talkin' aboot," he said. "Ye neednae think tae play aff ony o' yer tricks on me, boy. A didnae hurt a hair o' Corney's heid, an' A'm no sich a fule as to believe that you're Harry O'Neill. Noo watch yersel'; we hae law in the country."

"I shall not attempt to establish my identity to your satisfaction," replied Harry, "nor shall I bandy further words with you. Listen to me, Ben! The whole country can bear testimony to the fact that when Corney O'Neill was old and frail and dying, you would have thrown him out upon a ditch but for the interference of his neighbours. As for your laws, man, I despise them! You may have *laws*, but there is no JUSTICE in the land when *you* are allowed to pollute society with your presence. But there shall be justice now! Ben, I have come to kill you; I have, as there's a God in Heaven!"

There was no mistaking Harry's look and tone. Ben felt that the avenger stood before him, and again his heart seemed to congeal in the clutch of an icy hand. In an instant he saw his position, and a thousand thoughts flashed through his mind. His eye was fixed upon that of Harry O'Neill and he felt powerless to withdraw it. He seemed to have stood thus for hours though it was only for a few seconds. Harry's voice broke the spell—

"Get me a rope," he shouted hoarsely, "That I may hang you like the dog you are!"

Harry now appeared to have lost all self-control, and to be possessed alone by one desire—that of destroying the creature whom he regarded as his father's murderer. Ben felt that he must defend himself.

"Get me a rope, I say!" repeated Harry. As he spoke he turned his head and scanned the floor as though in search of the article for which he asked. This was Ben's opportunity and he embraced it. With a sudden movement he seized his stick and raised it above his head. But Harry had turned to face him, and turned too, just in the nick of time. Quick as lightning he swerved his head, and the blow came down upon his left shoulder with terrific force. Had it struck his head the blow would have been a fatal one. The next instant the two men were locked in each other's arms, struggling each for the mastery, and each conscious that the vanquished one must die. The fight was fierce, but it was of brief duration. Ben had flung away his stick and was struggling to get hold of Harry's throat. They rushed hither and thither, stamping their feet upon the floor, breathing heavily, but uttering not a word. Then there was a heavy fall! Harry's feet had slipped upon the damp floor and he went down with Ben on the top of him. And now his throat was in the clutch of Ben's muscular hands. Half stunned by the fall, Harry for a moment lay still, glaring in the face of his antagonist. Ben's heart beat wildly. He loosed his right hand and plunging it into the pocket of his jacket drew forth a huge clasp-knife, the blade of which he strove to open with his teeth. But Harry had recovered from his momentary bewilderment. With a swift movement he wrested Ben's left hand from his throat, flung him off, and rolled over upon him. Then, partly rising, he knelt upon the bailiff's breast. Thus they remained for fully a minute, Ben evidently worn out submitting to his fate whatever it might be; Harry seeking to recover his breath before completing his deed of vengeance. At length he spoke—

"Now, Ben Hanlon!" he hissed through his teeth, "it has been a duel after all; you did your best to kill me, but you failed. Now I shall kill you, not with a rope, nor with cudgel or a knife, but with this!"

And so saying he drew from his hip pocket a revolver and held it before Ben's eyes.

"Look at it," he said. "I little thought it was to be so applied."

"Mercy!" growled Ben; "let me leev; A din what wuz wrang, A know that; but forgie me an' A'll serve ye as lang as A leev."

Great beads of cold sweat rolled down his face; his eyes seemed starting from their sockets, and he lay without attempting to make a single movement.

"Seek mercy elsewhere," hissed Harry; "you showed none and none shall you receive."

There was a sharp click as Harry raised the hammer of the pistol and pressed the muzzle of it against the bailiff's ear.

CHAPTER XIX

BEN'S RESCUE

IT will be remembered that Widow Hunter urged Dominie Harvey to follow Harry O'Neill and endeavour to prevent him doing mischief to Black Ben. The worthy Dominie lost no time in donning his hat, picking up his stick, and starting off in pursuit of his old pupil. But the schoolmaster was unaccustomed to rapid walking. He was in the habit, when going from one place to another, of stepping slowly and with the utmost precision, his head bent forward, his eyes fixed as though he were engaged in the mental solution of some grave knotty problem, one hand placed in his bosom, the other holding his stout stick. But upon this occasion, the man's whole nature seemed to have undergone a change as remarkable as it was sudden. With all the speed which his old limbs possessed he pushed forward, and the violent exercise quickly produced its natural effects. Perspiration began to ooze from every pore, and the Dominie, passing his walking stick under his left arm, drew from his pocket a huge handkerchief of many colours and proceeded to wipe his steaming head and face.

Just as he approached Squire Brown's loaning or avenue, Miss Brown passed through the gate, dressed in her travelling costume. The sudden appearance of the Dominie, his hurried manner and agitated looks, startled her not a little. Darting forward, lightly as a fawn, she laid her daintily gloved hand upon his arm, and enquired—

"My dear sir, what has happened to distress you?"

But the Dominie's exertion and alarm had almost deprived him of his remarkable power of speech, and for the space of a moment he stood, with open mouth, panting and gazing stupidly at the fair face before him. But, as he looked, his expression of countenance changed, and a flash of pleased relief shot from his eyes. Then he found voice—

"Come with me and I'll tell you;" he gasped; "hurry, Miss there's no time to be lost."

Thus addressed, the fair girl turned without an instant's hesitation, placed her arm in that of the Dominie, and strove to the best of her ability to keep pace with the rapid, awkward strides. Then he, as best he could, told her what happened; of the unexpected arrival of Harry O'Neill; of the manner in which he received the tidings of his father's death and of his abrupt departure for Ben's quarters.

"But surely Harry cannot mean to commit any violence," said Miss Brown.

"I fear he does, Miss; God grant Ben may not be there, or that we may arrive in time. If we do, your presence will restrain him, I am sure."

Nothing more was said. It pained the Dominie to speak, such was his exhaustion, and the young lady shared his excitement and alarm. At length she spoke—

"You are tired. Dominie," she said; "let me run forward, as time may be precious."

"Yes do," gasped the old man, and she darted forward at a rapid run. The distance was short, and was speedily traversed. Just as Harry had placed the pistol at Ben's ear Annie Brown stood upon the threshold, her figure obscuring the light. Her shrill scream arrested Harry's hand. He started to his feet and glanced at the fair apparition which had so suddenly appeared. Then he quietly slipped the deadly weapon into his pocket, and stood with downcast head, as though ashamed of the position in which he had been found.

A brief silence followed. Ben lay upon his back, white as a corpse, and as though he momently expected the leaden messenger to crash through his brain; the squire's daughter remained at the open door, and pale and trembling; Harry stood abashed and apparently confounded by his mad outburst of temper. The appearance of the Dominie broke the silence.

"Let me in, dear," he said to Miss Brown, and that lady stepping to one side, the Dominie entered. At a glance he saw how matters stood.

"Why Harry, man, what's this?" he cried. "Did you think so little of yourself as to soil your honest hands upon this fellow?" Then turning to Ben, with a motion that indicated a strong desire to kick the bailiff, he said—"Get up, Ben! that is if every bone in your body has not been broken. Davey Morrow won't get an order for your coffin yet."

Ben turned over slowly, and with an anxious glance at Harry O'Neill as though doubting the safety of obeying the Dominie's command. But Harry heeded him not, and he rose to his feet with an evident air of relief.

By this time Harry had somewhat regained his composure. Raising his hat and bowing to Miss Brown, he said, in a voice that trembled—

"I am sorry that I should have caused you alarm. You would not blame me did you know the circumstances. Your arrival has prevented me from staining my hands with blood, and this cowardly ruffian shall escape for the present."

Harry had not recognised in the lady who stood before him the little girl for whom, in his boyhood, he had gathered bunches of wild flowers and performed countless little acts of gallantry; he knew not that he was watched by the soft blue eyes the memory of which had haunted him during all his absence from the land of his birth—he only knew that a lady's presence demanded some apology for the position in which he had been surprised. Ben spoke next—

"It wuz weel ye cummed in at the time ye did, mem," he said.

"If ye hadnae, my brains wud a been blowed oot afore noo, for that mad fella railly meent tae murder me. A'll awa an' sweer a 'refermashin' afore Squire Leslie, so A wull."

"You'll do nothing of the kind, fellow!" exclaimed the Dominie, bringing his stick down on the floor with a loud thud. "You may thank your stars that Harry did not shoot you; and still I don't know, Ben; shooting's decenter than hanging, and I believe you'll be hung some day!"

"Yer complementary the day, Dominie," growled Ben, who had now partially recovered from his fright.

Then the Dominie turned to Harry and said—

"Harry, my boy, do you not recognise our dear, good friend, the Squire's daughter, Miss Brown?"

Harry started violently.

"Can it be possible!" he exclaimed. "Oh, Miss Brown, I little thought our first meeting would be like this." He covered his face with his hands, and stood silent for several moments. Then he quietly passed from Ben's hut. When he was outside he turned, and said—

"Miss Brown do not condemn me for what I have done. Wait until I tell you what I have suffered. Then, perhaps, you will forgive me and allow me to shake hands with you." And so saying, he replaced his hat upon his head and walked away.

Ere the sound of Harry's footsteps had died in the distance, Ben's rage burst forth. The presence of his master's daughter did not check the torrent of oaths and vows of vengeance that fell from his lips. He would have vengeance; he would have Harry banished from the country to which he had just returned; he would show this mad-brained adventurer that there was law in County Down.

The Dominie stood by quietly, enjoying an occasional pinch of snuff, and saying nothing until Ben seemed to have nothing more to say. Then he brought all his eloquence into play. He pledged his word that Harry O'Neill would never more molest him; he dilated upon the great provocation which had led to this encounter; pointed to Ben's unpopularity in the neighbourhood, and which unpopularity would only be increased tenfold did he make an effort to have Harry punished for what was, after all, merely a natural outburst of indignation. And the Squire's daughter, watching her opportunity, had also a word to say. She told Ben that her father was greatly incensed against him for his late conduct; that one word from her would secure his instant dismissal, and that unless a promise were now given that no more would be said of the affair—on condition of Harry's promising to abstain from further violence—she would say that word and have him dismissed.

And Ben gave the required promise. He promised because he felt that by doing so he would best serve his own interests. But he did it reluctantly, and in his heart he vowed to seek vengeance upon Harry O'Neill.

Then Annie Brown, taking the Dominie's arm, went away from the hut. As she stepped out into the clear bright sunshine, she gave a sigh of relief, and as she walked along by the Dominie's side she listened with a pleased look upon her fair face to the old man's enthusiastic descriptions and glowing opinions of Harry O'Neill, and felt thankful in her heart that she had been instrumental in saving Harry from embruing his hands in a fellow-creature's blood.

She did not dream that the day was not far distant when she would wish that the bullet from Harry's pistol had been allowed to pierce the brain of as vile a ruffian as ever lived in her fair county.

CHAPTER XX

THE COURSE OF TRUE LOVE NEVER RUNS SMOOTH

MONTHS had passed away since the events which have been recorded. The golden grain was waving on the broad plains of the fair Ards, and the heart of the husbandman rejoiced in view of a plenteous harvest. Spring had succeeded winter and autumn had followed upon summer. The changes in the affairs of those who figure in my story were in many instances trifling, in others they were more marked. This was especially the case with Harry O'Neill. He seemed to have forgotten his enmity towards Black Ben. Perhaps it was because other thoughts engrossed his mind. He had erected a handsome tablet at the head of his parents' grave, and he still wore a badge of mourning upon his hat. As yet he had no settled place of abode and apparently no object in life. Much of his time was spent in Newtownards, visiting his old acquaintances; Greyabbey, Carrowdore, and Millisle claimed much of his attention, the Mills in the latter place being a favourite resort. He was a regular visitor at Widow Hunter's, and between him and Taylor, the schoolmaster, a warm friendship had sprung up.

I have said that certain thoughts occupied Harry's mind. He was in love, and the object of his passion was, as might be expected, the squire's daughter. Some days after the encounter with the bailiff, Harry called upon Miss Brown. He was received with a certain amount of shyness, yet his welcome was a cordial one. The interview was short. With considerable embarrassment he accounted for his attack upon Black Ben and craved forgiveness. This was readily given, and Miss Brown begged him to dismiss the subject from his mind. When he left it was with the promise that he would soon return to relate his travels and adventures. He was not long until he availed himself of the permission given. This time he was introduced to the squire, who chanced to be in an agreeable mood, and the three had tea together. Squire Brown seemed pleased with the bronzed face and manly figure of his guest, and expressed the pleasure he would feel in seeing him often. And Harry was at the squire's often—very often. He did not always see the squire on these occasions, nor did he wish to. Many and pleasant were the hours spent in the company of Annie Brown, and now all reserve was thrown aside. Over and over again had he told her how in his wanderings by sea and land one fair face with its soft blue eyes had been ever before him; attending him like some good angel; cheering him in his hours of despondency; nerving him when his heart was ready to fall. He had told her how when fortune smiled upon him, his chief happiness arose from the hope that his boyish anticipations might be realised; he looked upon the golden ore which came to him in such profusion as the means by which he would obtain as his wife the fair little creature whose image was ever before him.

"And did you really think that gold would win me?" asked Annie.

"No and yes," answered Harry; "I knew that in your eyes gold would be as so much dross, and that your heart must be won by something far more precious; but I also knew that your father was a proud man and one who would never consent to wed his daughter to a penniless adventurer. It was this that made me value gold far beyond its intrinsic worth. And then, too, I was fortunate in other respects. The lot which I worked was divided with a brave, good fellow, who had shared my fortune for years. He was a scholar, the son of a gentleman, smitten like myself with the gold fever, and during the long winter nights he taught me much that I could never otherwise have known. And

THE COURSE OF TRUE LOVE

I was an apt pupil, Annie; for the same motive which led me to dig for gold impelled me to seek after the culture of a mind otherwise rude. Often did I think of those lines which Dominie Harvey was so fond of quoting—

> "Till Education lend her aid, unknown
>   The brightest talents lie—a common stone;
>   By her fair hands when fashioned, the new mind
>   Rises with lustre, polished and refined."

"Well, Harry, you have done your teacher credit. Where is he now?"

"On his way home, I expect; you may see him some day."

The young lovers sat in Annie's parlour one lovely harvest afternoon, chatting in their usual strain. Annie played and sang some of Harry's favourite airs; then turning round, with a coy glance at the handsome face beside her, said—

"Haven't you something to sing, Harry?"

"To be sure, I have, Annie, and it just seems as though I had written it specially for you."

Then in a fine rich voice, Harry sang the following verses:—

> "Oh, I'm lonely to-night, love, without you,
>   And I sigh for one glance of your eye;
> For sure there's a charm, love, about you,
>   Whenever I know you are nigh;
> Like the beam of the star, when 'tis smiling,
>   Is the glance which your eye can't conceal;
> And your voice is so sweet and beguiling
>   That I love you, sweet Nora O'Neal.
>
> Oh! the nightingale sings in the wild-wood,
>   As if every note that he knew

Was learned from your sweet voice in childhood,
    To remind me, sweet Nora, of you;
But I think, love, so often about you,
    And you don't know how happy I feel,
But I'm lonely to-night, love, without you,
    My darling, sweet Nora O'Neal.

Oh! why should I weep tears of sorrow?
    Or why then let hope lose its place?
Won't I meet you, my darling, to-morrow,
    And smile on your beautiful face?
Will you meet me? Oh, say will you meet me,
    With a kiss at the foot of the lane?
And I'll promise whenever you greet me,
    That I'll never be lonely again!"

"Now, Annie," he said, at the close of the song, "doesn't it just seem written for you?"

Annie did not answer; she seemed busy with her embroidery.

"There's just one thing about it that I don't like," he continued; "your name isn't 'Nora'; the song should be to 'Annie'."

"And my name is Brown, *not* O'Neill," said Annie, demurely.

"True," said Harry; "but one day it will be, won't it?"

Annie was again silent. Harry went on—

"Your father suspects nothing as yet; even the neighbours, talkative as they are, have not whispered a word regarding us. But I must know my fate at once. I shall call upon your father to-morrow and ask him for my darling. How will he receive me, do you think?"

Annie shook her head sadly as she answered—

"My father is a peculiar man, Harry; and my heart tells me that he will refuse. I feel a strange foreboding of dark days to come."

THE COURSE OF TRUE LOVE

"Nonsense, dearest," murmured Harry, as he slid his arm round the fair girl's waist; "what dark days can there be in store for you? Why should your father refuse to let you wed me? I shall seek an early opportunity to see him."

The opportunity came to Harry sooner than he expected. A step sounded in the hall; Annie glided off to her piano, the door opened and Squire Brown stepped into the parlour.

"Good evening, Mr. O'Neill," he said pleasantly, extending his hand to Harry.

Harry was somewhat embarrassed by the sudden entrance of the squire, but was not noticed by the latter, who sat down in an old arm chair for the purpose, apparently, of having a chat. Annie slipped noiselessly from the room.

"Well I suppose you find the old place dull," said the squire.

"By no means, sir," replied Harry; "on the contrary I am delighted to be once more amongst my old friends."

"Very unusual," remarked the squire; "most young fellows after seeing the world, as you have, can't settle down in their former quarters, but lead a roving life to the end of the chapter."

Thus they chatted for some time. The squire was in excellent humour, and Harry, whose nature ever impelled him to act promptly, whatever the situation or circumstances might be, felt that now was his time.

"Squire," he said, "there is a subject upon which I wish to speak with you." His voice trembled, and his heart beat violently.

"What is that?" asked the squire, wheeling round suddenly in his chair so as to face Harry. The reply came with sudden abruptness.

"I love your daughter; may I marry her?"

The expression of the squire's face was indescribable. Anger and amazement seemed struggling for the mastery. For several moments he gazed into Harry's face in speechless wonder. Then he started to his feet.

"Love my daughter!" he exclaimed. "Want to marry her! What the devil do you mean, sir?"

Harry was now perfectly composed.

"I have told you what I mean, sir;" he replied quietly.

"Have you told my daughter of this?" demanded the squire.

"Certainly."

"And you have her permission to speak to me?"

"I have."

The squire sank again into his chair breathing heavily.

"What is your objection to me?" asked Harry.

The squire did not answer, and Harry continued—

"Squire, I love your daughter and she loves me. I am rich; and I can make her happy and independent; I—."

"Stop man!" shouted the squire, again jumping to his feet. "What do I care for your wealth? There are other things to be looked to. Consider your birth, your social position. What are you man? Why you are a mere—."

"*Son of the Sod*" cried Harry, in turn springing to his feet, and concluding the squire's sentence for him. "Mark my words, Squire, I have won your daughter's love, and I'll make her my wife, too!"

The expression of the Squire's face was absolutely frightful, and for a moment he was speechless. Then he opened the door and pointing to it with his finger, exclaimed—

"Quit my house, sir, and never darken my door again!"

CHAPTER XXI

CUTTING THE CHURN

IT is some time since we were in the neighbourhood of "The Hill," where matters were going on as usual, and where Johnnie Hunter continued to pay numerous visits to his sweetheart, Jeannie Banks. The presence of Taylor and Hunter at "The Hill" upon the night of the Carrowdore ball had never been discovered by the father or mother of the girls, but the young people themselves had enjoyed many a hearty laugh on the subject.

It is a glorious harvest day. The sickles are busy cutting down the rich, golden grain; and the reapers as they bend under the scorching rays of the sun, pause now and then to draw from a large jar a cooling and refreshing draught of whey. On "The Hill" farm there remains but one handful of corn, and an interesting ceremony is about to take place—that of cutting the churn. I have said that many of the Widow's neighbours assisted her in the cultivation of her little farm. In return for this Johnnie Hunter was always ready to give a day's work willingly, and accordingly we now find him shearing at "The Hill." The farm labourers have stretched themselves to rest upon the fresh, crisp stubble; and the handsome Jeannie, attired in a smart cotton gown and snowy apron, stands fanning herself with her broad-brimmed straw hat. Meanwhile young Hunter is preparing "the churn." Laying hold of the handful of standing corn he plaits it as a girl would plait her hair, and then with a stout stalk he ties it at the top. Next, he steps off a distance of several paces and marks the spot, drawing a deep rut in the soft earth with the heel of his boot. The reapers rise, and sickle in hand gather around.

"Ir ye a' reddy?" asked Hunter; "noo fair throwin', mind ye, and Jeannie gets the first shot; cum Jeannie, stan tae the line."

Thus accosted, the handsome girl stepped forward, with sparkling eye and smiling face. Balancing her reaping hook deftly for an instant in her shapely hand, she threw it in the direction of the churn. It was a well-aimed stroke, for the keen-edged implement struck the object a few inches above the ground and cut through several of the stalks of grain.

A loud cheer followed, and then the others took their turn. Hunter came last, and his efforts completed the work, his sickle cutting completely through the grain. Amid the cheers of the party Johnnie placed the "churn" round Jeannie's neck and claimed his expected fee—a kiss. For this, however, there was a sharp struggle, but in the end Johnnie was victorious. All then proceeded to the house where the good mistress, assisted by her daughter Mary Ann, had been making preparations to receive them. There was an abundant supply of tea, whiskey, buttered oat-cake and cheese, and for fully half an hour unbounded mirth prevailed. Meantime the "churn" had been suspended in a prominent part of the house, and the health of Mr. and Mrs. Banks had been proposed and duly honoured.

As the party left to complete their day's work, Mrs. Banks reminded them in cheery tones—

"Noo, we'll haud the churn the morrow nicht an' ye maun a' be here. Sweep up the barn for a dance and see aboot a fiddler."

"We wull dae that!" was the ready response, and the reapers trooped out, brimful of merriment. They did not perceive the dark cloud which was looming in the horizon of their quiet and peaceful surroundings.

CHAPTER XXII

MURDER

AT the Big House everything seemed enveloped in gloom. Since the evening upon which Harry O'Neill had been so unceremoniously turned out of doors the Squire had neither quitted his room nor spoken to his daughter. And Annie, poor girl, was half distracted. Her eyes were red with weeping; her heart felt ready to burst. Dark forebodings filled her mind; night came, but to her it brought no rest, morning dawned, but when it came no joy. She had not seen Harry since, but she had heard from him daily by the hand of a trusty friend. Harry's letters were very welcome to Annie, yet they failed to afford her comfort. True, they were full of endearing language, breathing the love of a manly heart and noble nature, but a spirit of wild despair and fierce anger pervaded them, and Annie feared that something dreadful should happen. Night after night, in accordance with a private arrangement, a letter from Harry had safely reached her hand until the day of the churn-cutting at "The Hill" farm. The evening deepened into night, but her faithful messenger came not. Once she thought she saw his figure approaching, stopping for a few minutes and then hurrying away. Again, her heart beat rapidly as a cautious foot sounded upon the gravel beneath her window. That, too, passed away, and in a despairing mood she flung herself upon her bed. How long she lay thus she could never tell. Sleep had seized upon her, a broken, troubled sleep, from which she awoke to hear the stroke of the old eight-day clock which stood in the hall. It was the hour of midnight. Scarcely had the sound of the last sonorous stroke died away than a shriek which chilled Annie's blood rang through the house. It was repeated again and again as she sprang from her bed and stood like one in a dream. Each scream sounded nearer, there was a rush of feet up the staircase, a hand clutched at the handle of her door, and the well-known voice of Jane, her servant maid, cried aloud—

"Murder, Murder! The Squire's kilt!"

The startling words aroused Annie from her stupor. Dashing to the door she opened it and Jane fell fainting in her arms. With almost superhuman strength she dragged the poor girl to a sofa, and stretching her upon it procured some water and dashed it on her face, restoring her to consciousness. By this time two of the men farm-servants who slept on the premises, roused by the screams, came upon the scene. Jane was questioned, but all she could say was—

"The Squire's in his room murdered."

Summoning up all the courage she possessed, Annie lifted her lamp and begged the men to accompany her, which they did. The Squire's apartment was on the ground floor, and when the four terror-stricken creatures reached it they witnessed a horrible sight. The Squire lay upon the floor in a pool of blood, his head and face fearfully bruised, mangled and gory. To all appearance a brutal murder had been committed. Annie swooned away on seeing her father, while the men looked on in speechless wonder.

"Run for help!" cried Jane.

Both men turned, half-dazed, to obey her command.

"Ye neednae baith gang," cried Jane; "stae yin o' ye here. Wheesht, A think A hear a car?"

Jane's quick ear had not deceived her. When the man went out a car was passing which he hailed. The driver, Johnnie Tennent, Carrowdore, pulled up at once.

"Who are you and what do you want?" asked a pleasant voice.

"I want help!" gasped the man; "sumbuddy haes brauken in here an' murdered Squire Broon."

"Good God! Whitla, what's this?" cried one of the passengers, and so saying he jumped from the car and ran towards the house. The other followed more leisurely, for he was a man of immense size. The presence of these travellers seemed providential, they were no other than Doctors Whitla of Newtownards and Shaw of Greyabbey, who had been summoned to meet a local doctor in consultation upon a critical case, and they were now returning home.

The two medical men, on entering the room, took in all at a glance. With the assistance of the men they lifted the Squire and placed him upon the table. A hasty inspection showed them that he still lived.

"Come, good woman, bestir yourself!" said Doctor Whitla to Jane, "get some warm water, sponges if you have them, and some old linen—a sheet, anything. Ha! what's this?" he continued, as his eye fell upon the unconscious form of Annie stretched upon the sofa.

One of the men told what had happened. The doctor drew a small phial from a hand-bag which he carried, and administered a restorative which had quickly the desired effect.

"My father," she murmured, as she unclosed her eyes.

"He still lives, Miss Brown," whispered the doctor.

"Oh, who are you?" she exclaimed, starting up.

"I am Doctor Whitla, and here is Doctor Shaw, both friends to you and your father. Now, my poor girl, you must go and leave us."

"Oh, won't you save my father!" she pleaded, while the tears coursed down her cheeks.

"Yes, if it's God's will; but every moment is precious; assist your maid in carrying out our directions."

"I will, doctor; thank God that you are here."

As Annie said these words she left the room and the good doctor went to assist his colleague in his endeavours to restore to life and consciousness the man who, to less experienced eyes, must have seemed to be beyond all earthly assistance.

CHAPTER XXIII

WHO DID IT?

DURING the whole of that eventful night both doctors remained with the patient so unexpectedly placed in their hands. By their directions a temporary bed had been erected in the room in which the squire had been attacked. Stretched upon that bed he lay, still and silent as a corpse. The bloody stains had been washed away, and part of the clothing removed. The man lived and breathed, but consciousness had not returned. The sun had risen in all its glory, and its rays, struggling in through the small diamond-shaped window panes, made the bruised and swollen face appear terrible ghastly. Dr. Whitla sat at one side of the bed; Dr. Shaw at the other. Near to them stood Annie, in an agony of grief, her eyes one moment fixed upon the disfigured features of her father, and the next scanning the doctors' faces to see what she might read therein. She could learn nothing there. At length Dr. Whitla rose to his feet and consulted his watch. Then, in a low tone, he said to his companion—

"Shaw, I must go; I really can't stay longer. I'll send those things to you that you require."

"Very well," replied Dr. Shaw.

"Oh, are you going to leave him?" asked Annie.

The doctor, with a motion of his hand, enjoined silence, and then stepping towards the door of the apartment he beckoned to the young lady to follow him. Annie was by his side in the hall in a moment.

"Now, my dear girl," he said kindly, "you must be as calm and collected as is possible for you to be under these very distressing circumstances. Have you a man here who can drive me to Newtownards?"

"Certainly, doctor."

"Then the sooner I am on my way the better for all of us. Send for him."

Annie ran to the kitchen.

"Jane," she said to the servant, who was sitting before the fire like one dazed, "run out for John M'Cluskey the gardener; tell him to put the grey mare in the car and drive Dr. Whitla to Newtownards."

On coming back she found the doctor intently examining the fastenings of the hall door. He turned on hearing Annie's footstep, and there was a look of grave thought upon his large good-natured face as he said—

"I'm not much of a detective, my dear, but it strikes me that last night's work was not done by a stranger."

"Oh, Doctor, why do you say so?"

"Well, I can scarcely tell you," he answered, "but the murdering villain must be discovered. He's a sharp fellow the Sergeant of Police in Newtownards. I have a wonderful confidence in his abilities, and I'll send him out here by your car the moment I arrive. I shall also send Dr. Shaw what he requires; he has promised me not to leave your father until he finds he can be of no further use, and I shall send a man to Greyabbey to take charge of his dispensary. At present we can form no opinion about the result, but you know that while there is life there is hope. Your father may recover; it is quite possible."

"Oh, I trust he shall," said Annie, wringing her hands.

"Well, as I said before," the doctor went on, "keep yourself calm and collected; when the Sergeant comes out, answer all his questions and supply him with whatever he may require. Let nothing be touched till he comes. That stick lying in the room with blood-stains upon it may afford a clue. Ha! here is the car; good morning, my dear."

The good doctor stepped out, clambered lazily on to the car,

WHO DID IT?

settled himself comfortably, and gave the word to start.

The people of the Ards are early risers, and long ere the doctor had started—early though the hour was—scores of workers were in the harvest fields. Some were cutting grain, others stooking, but the doctor could not fail to observe that the harvesters did not work with their accustomed diligence, and that as he passed along they eyed him with more than ordinary interest.

"Suppose they've heard all about it," muttered the doctor; "shouldn't wonder but the very hand which sought to murder old Brown is busy reaping God's harvest. Drive on, my man; time is precious."

M'Cluskey touched the mare lightly with his whip, and she started off at a rattling pace.

Meantime the news had spread like wildfire. Nothing else was talked of in the fields, the farmyards and the homes, and the question went from lip to lip—

"Wha cud dae it?"

And the invariable answer, accompanied by an emphatic shake of the head, was—

"A'm shair A dae not ken."

Indeed nothing could have surprised the tenantry more. Squire Brown was far from enjoying popularity, yet he was very highly respected in the neighbourhood, and was never known to have incurred the deadly enmity of anyone. Had his bailiff, Black Ben, been found brutally beaten or murdered, no one would have wondered; few would have expressed regret.

And no one seemed to be more shocked and indignant than Ben himself. When the news had been communicated to him during the night he was, for a brief space, apparently dumbfounded, then he waxed furious and hurled the most fearful anathemas at the head of the would-be murderer. He at once rose and dressed; ransacked by the light of a lantern, barns, byres, stables and other office houses, but whether in hope of finding some person or persons concealed there, or that he wished to see what, if any, property had been made off with, he did not condescend to inform anyone. Jane, the maidservant, was the only person with whom Ben talked upon the subject, and with her he conversed freely. His search over, he ensconced himself in the kitchen by the fire, so as to be in readiness should his services be required. But no one called upon him. The doctors were busy with the Squire, and Miss Brown and Jane were similarly occupied, the latter passing frequently from the Squire's room to the kitchen. Ben learned from Jane that the Squire, though evidently left for dead, still lived. The news affected him strangely, considering his rough, unfeeling nature. But then Ben had always been devoted to the Squire, serving him, as far as observers could judge, with singular fidelity.

"An' he's no deid!" he gasped, with a sudden change of countenance which seemed to express relief. "Hing by them, Jane; hing by them, and bring me a' the news ye can."

But Jane had no further news to report, and Ben wandered about the premises, with lowering brows and his hands in his pockets, speaking to no one.

Considerably before twelve o'clock the police sergeant and three of his men arrived at the Big House. The sergeant, having had a brief interview with Miss Brown, at once proceeded with his investigations. He speedily discovered what, until now, had been unobserved, that a strong tin box had been broken open. It contained a number of deeds and documents, some blocks of cheque books, a cheque book partly used, and a cash box. The latter was empty. Upon the table there lay a ledger containing the Squire's rent roll and other accounts. A stick had been found upon the floor by the doctors; it was a stout ash plant, and was smeared with blood. Dr. Shaw informed the sergeant that the wounds upon the Squire's head and face had apparently been inflicted by a blunt instrument, such, for instance, as the ash plant in question. Miss Brown, in reply to the sergeant, informed him that her father kept his money in the cash box, which was deposited in the deed box, but she had no knowledge of what sum, if any, the cash box might have contained. Thus, for so far, the only clue, and it was a slight one, was the ash plant, evidently left behind by the culprit.

The sergeant, accompanied by his men, inspected the entire premises, without and within, now and then making notes in a small memorandum book. Fully two hours were thus spent, after which the sergeant placed two of his men upon the premises with instructions, privately conveyed, and left the house accompanied by his third man. He spent the entire day in scouring the country, calling at every house; enquiring from the people whether they had lately seen any suspicious looking characters in the neighbourhood, and occasionally noting the information received. It was almost night when he returned to the Squire's house, and he appeared to be both fatigued and dispirited. He had a further interview with the doctor and Miss Brown, after which, having partaken of some refreshments, he rose to leave. As he did so, Black Ben passed the window.

"Isn't that your bailiff?" the sergeant enquired of Miss Brown.

"It is," she replied, "Ben Hanlon."

"He should know a good deal about your father's affairs," remarked the sergeant, "you might call him in—but stay, I'll just pick him up myself," and so saying he went out.

Ben was on his way to his own quarters, and had almost reached them when, hearing the steady, measured tread of the policeman, he turned round.

"Good evening, sergeant," he said.

"Good evening, Hanlon; this is a bad business about poor Squire Brown."

"A terble business, sir; is he likely tae get over it dae ye think?"

"The doctor has just told me that he may live, but he fears that he will never recover his senses."

"Hoo that?" queried Ben, watching the sergeant closely from beneath his beetling brows.

"His skull is so beaten that the doctors believe the brain must be injured to such an extent that he may be an imbecile. Poor man! it might be better for him that he should die."

"Ir ye cummin' in, sergeant?" asked Ben, as he opened the door.

"Yes; I want a word with you, perhaps you can give me some help."

The sergeant carried in his hand the blood-stained ash plant, rolled up in a piece of newspaper.

Ten minutes afterwards the sergeant and Ben emerged from the house and started off towards the main road at a rapid pace. A look of satisfaction was upon the face of the sergeant; Ben's countenance indicated a mingled expression of fear and triumph.

They were bound for the residence of the nearest magistrate.

CHAPTER XXIV

ON THE TRACK

WE shall not follow the sergeant and his companion, but shall, instead, peep in at The Hill, where the "churn" was being held amid boundless fun and frolic. Some thirty persons were present, but these included the members of the household, and the farm servants. Several neighbouring farmers, with their families, had been invited, and the house was inconveniently crowded. The day had been one of bustle and confusion at The Hill. From early morning, cooking, scrubbing, and cleaning had been going on. Some inmates of the poultry yard had fallen victims to the occasion and now lay quietly awaiting dissection. The supper table, laid out in the largest room which the house could boast, fairly groaned beneath the weight of the good things crowded upon it. A person unaccustomed to such scenes would doubtless have marvelled at the profusion displayed; the huge piles of oatcake, and every variety of home made bread; the ponderous cheese; the plates of butter; hams, fowl, and other tempting and savoury dishes. Truly a regiment of hungry soldiers might there have banqueted to the full.

Sharp to time the guests arrive. The men sit down in the kitchen, where a huge turf fire burns under the old lum, and the women folks are escorted "doon the hoose" to lay aside their bonnets and shawls and, if so inclined, sharpen their appetites with "a wee half yin."

At length Mrs. Banks announces "Noo, weans, yer supper's ready!" and there is a general rising. Soon the supper room is crowded, but the lack of elbow room is good-naturedly endured. There is an indescribable bustle and rattling of chairs before all are seated. Mrs. Banks, in all the glory of a black silk dress and showy cap, directs her husband in his duties as host, and she herself is far from idle. Her tongue never rests—

"Cum Jennie, whaur's the hard breid? Be smert woman and pit it roon. Mary Ann, see that Mistress Jamison's takin' sumthin' there. Noo, weans, make yersels at hame an' dinnae be scaured tae pit forrit yer han. Hoots, Mistress Broon, pit butter on yer breid woman. There's plenty mair fur the churnin."

Thus did the good woman chatter away, while her husband and daughters kept piling up the plates of their guests. Shyness was visible at first, but it speedily vanished, and the substantial viands rapidly dwindled down amid the clatter of knives and forks, the loud buzz of conversation, and the heartiest shouts of laughter. Next came the punch and "sumthing saft for the lasses." As might be expected, the hilarity speedily increased. Song succeeded song, and story followed upon story. Our old friend the Dominie was there, and right well did he enjoy himself. By and by the young people adjourned to the barn for a dance, but the older people sat chatting over their punch. Johnnie Hunter and his sweetheart Jeannie led off the dance, and the proceedings were of the merriest description. There were light hearts and light heels in the barn that night. What did any of the dancers know of care? Absolutely nothing. Life might be somewhat monotonous with them, but it was untroubled. Young Hunter seemed perfectly delirious with joy as he whirled his partner round the barn, and never had Jeannie looked so charming.

But people tire of dancing as well as of everything else, and by and by an adjournment was made to the kitchen where a variety of games were engaged in. Blind man's buff, Monk and Nun, the Postman, forfeits, riddles, and storytelling passed the hours pleasantly. The Dominie and Johnnie Hunter were vieing with each other as to who could tell the "biggest bummer," (i.e., the greatest lie) a practice quite common on such occasions.

ON THE TRACK

The Dominie told how when standing at the Newtownards Flood Gates he counted a flock of chickens at Castle Espie, and Johnnie had retaliated by declaring that from the same place he saw a man named Bunt selling herrings to a woman in Donaghadee, and getting a bad sixpence in payment of same. Every story, though hackneyed by frequent repetition, was loudly applauded. The Dominie was getting the best of it and had just told a very tall shooting story which seemed to cap the climax but Johnnie was not to be outdone in the sporting line at all events. He began—

"The last time A wuz oot in Australia (Hunter had never been farther from home than Belfast) A seen the biggest birds that iver A seen in my life. Ye talk aboot yer wild geese but they're jest like chittyrans compared wi' thon. Weel, they wur terble wild; mony a time they fleed ower my heid, but they waur miles heech. The mester tell't me that mony a time, in the early mornin', he had seen them sittin' on a big thorn hedge, and that if A wud watch my han' A micht get a shot at them. A tried it mony a time, but it wuz nae use; A niver cud get nearer them nor two hunner yerds. Yin day a pedler cummed roon; A wuz plewin, an' he jumped ower the dyke to shew me what he had in his box. A bocht a knife frae him an' lifted what A thocht wuz a tabaka box an' axed the price. He shewed me that it wuz fu' o' a thing like glue an' tell't me it wuz a gran' thing for catchin' birds wi'. He said sae muckle aboot it that A bocht a box thinking A wud try it on the big geese, as A ca'd them. That nicht A spread the hale o' it on the tap o' the thorn hedge an' A cudnae sleep a wink for thinkin' aboot it. A luckit oot the nixt mornin' at daylicht, an' behold ye, but there wuz the birds sittin' on the very place A put the glue. It wuznae lang till A wuz oot wi' the gun. They sut watchin' me till A wuz aboot twa hunner yerds aff them an' they made tae flee awa. But deil a bit o' them cud dae it. It made me lauch ower ocht, an' so A jest dannered forrit at my leisure till A wuznae mair nor fifty yerds aff them. A wush ye had heerd the flappin' o' their wings! A put the gun tae my shooder, but afore A cud study it they gied the maist unerthly yell iver A heerd an' awa they flew takin' aboot two perch o' the hedge an' dyke wi' them."

"Yer bate, Dominie yer bate!" cried half a dozen voices; "well din, Johnnie, but it's a wonner that yin didnae choke ye!"

There was a sharp rap at the door, evidently produced by a walking stick. Mary Ann Banks opened the door, and there stepped in the Sergeant of Police, two of his men, and Black Ben slinking in the rear.

"Which of you is Johnnie Hunter?" asked the Sergeant.

So sudden had been the interruption and so thunderstruck were the people at the appearance of the police that not one stirred or spoke.

"That's him!" said Ben Hanlon, stepping forward and pointing out Hunter.

The young man started to his feet.

"A'm Johnnie Hunter," he said; "wur ye wantin' me?"

"You are my prisoner!" said the Sergeant, laying his hand on Hunter's shoulder.

By this time the alarm had reached the supper room, and all crowded into the kitchen, consternation on every face. Poor Johnnie was speechless, and his sweetheart, rushing into another apartment, began to sob convulsively.

At last Johnnie found tongue—

"What hae a din?" he demanded.

The Sergeant looked at him steadily, and then amidst the most profound silence of the onlookers, he said, slowly and with painful distinctness—

"You are charged with the murder of Squire Brown!"

The scene which followed baffles description. The women screamed; the men pressed around the Sergeant assuring him that there must be some mistake. The clamour was frightful.

"Stand back, good people," said the Sergeant firmly but kindly; "I am sorry to disturb your pleasant evening, but duty, however disagreeable, must be performed."

He drew a pair of handcuffs from his pocket and quietly slipped them upon Johnnie's wrists. This act seemed to rouse the unhappy youth from the stupor into which he appeared to have fallen.

"It's a d—d lee," he shouted; "tell me wha says it till a teer the heart oot o' him." His eye fell on Ben.

"Was it HIM said it?" he gasped, struggling hard to reach the bailiff. But the policemen, at a nod from the Sergeant, placed themselves at either side of Hunter, and Ben slunk off towards the door.

"Hunter," said the Sergeant, "it is my duty to caution you that anything which you now say may hereafter be used against you."

"Me Murder the Squire!" exclaimed Hunter; "naebuddy here beleeves that; shair ye dinna, freens?" and he turned an appealing look round him.

"Na, no yin o' us!" cried several voices.

"Come, my man," said the Sergeant, "there's a car waiting; we must be off."

"My puir mither!" cried Johnnie, and on the recollection of his widowed parent his fortitude deserted him and he burst into tears.

Thus was he led out, and, helpless as a child, lifted upon the car. That night he was lodged in Newtownards bridewell.

CHAPTER XXV

THE PLOT THICKENS

MY readers will doubtless have surmised that Johnnie Hunter was arrested upon information supplied by Ben Hanlon. And such was the case. It will be remembered that the Sergeant of Police went into Ben's hut in quest of information.

"Tell me, Hanlon," said the Sergeant, "was the Squire in the habit of keeping much cash in the house?"

"Weel, A cud not tell ye that," answered Ben.

"Have you at any time seen much in his possession at the house?"

"Well there wuz times whun A gied him the fowks' rent that he micht a haen a wheen hunner pund."

The Sergeant cautiously unwrapped the stick which he had been carrying. It was a stout ash plant; to all appearance it had been but recently cut, and it was smeared with blood. He handed it to Ben, remarking as he did so—

"I would give something to know the owner of that."

Ben took the stick and looked at it closely. As he did so he gave a slight start. Then he rose and stepped to the door where he examined it minutely by the better light there afforded. Having completed the inspection he returned the stick to the Sergeant, with the remark, delivered in the most matter of fact tones—

"A can tell ye that, Sergint."

"Tell me what?" demanded the Sergeant, jumping to his feet.

"Wha the ash plant belangs tae," said Ben, in the same dry voice; "at ony rate A seen Johnnie Hunter cuttin' it in the plantin' aboot a fortnicht ago."

The Sergeant stood gazing at Ben as though he could scarce credit his ears.

THE PLOT THICKENS

"And who is this Hunter?" he asked, eagerly.

"Oh, he's no a terble guid yin; he's a son o' Weeda Hunter's that leevs doon the road there a bit."

"But look here, Ben, is there the slightest possibility of Hunter being concerned in this?"

Ben sat down, placed his coarse hands upon his knees, ejected a considerable quantity of tobacco juice, and looking fixedly at the Sergeant, said—

"A wudnae like tae dae onybuddy an ill turn, but it's my duty tae tell ye what A know, an' A may say that it micht niver a struck me had it no been that ye showed me that stick. Noo, a while back here a fella they ca' Harry O'Neill cummed hame frae the goold diggins, an' he throws his money aboot him like slate stanes. This fella an' young Hunter's a guid dale thegither, an' Hunter wul like tae be as flush of money as the tither, an' mair betoken he's coortin' a lass that he'll niver pit a ring on if he canna show up a bit o' money. Noo' Sergint, A heerd him myself yin day in Newtown sayin' that he wud rise the money *if he should rob the Squire fur it.*"

The Sergeant did not speak, but he listened attentively. Ben went on—

"A hae the oddest pert tae tell ye yit. This while back A hae seen Hunter jookin' aboot the Squire's place efter dark, an' A seen him there last nicht."

"At what time, Ben?"

"Weel it wud be efter ten o'clock."

"Did you speak to him?"

"A did not; whun he heerd my fut he jookit in amang the laurel bushes."

"And that's all you know?"

"Naethin else. There's mebbe no muckle in it."

"It strikes me there's a good deal in it," said the Sergeant. "Come along, Hanlon, I'll have a warrant for this young fellow's arrest before I'm very much older."

"Dinnae dae ocht rash," remonstrated Ben.

"Never fear, my man, come along."

And thus it happened that Johnnie Hunter was arrested on suspicion of having murdered and robbed Squire Brown. The commotion in the country was great; the excitement intense. No one would believe Hunter guilty, and no one displayed more indignation upon hearing the arrest than did the Squire's daughter. As for Johnnie's mother, she was frantic with grief, and presented a most pitiable spectacle. She refused to listen to consolation. Her eyes were swollen and red with weeping; she had wept until tears refused to come. Harry O'Neill bestirred himself in a practical fashion. After the first outbreak of astonishment and indignation, he set to work with all the energy he possessed. He employed one of the most eminent lawyers in Belfast to conduct Johnnie's defence before the Petty Sessions Court, and declared that, if necessary, he would spend his last shilling in establishing his friend's innocence. He did not know what a difficult task he had assigned himself.

CHAPTER XXVI

DR. SHAW

WHEN Squire Brown's daughter had somewhat recovered from the shock sustained to her nervous system, she devoted the most unremitting attention to her father and the good doctor who had so fortunately been at hand when the discovery of the Squire's condition had been made.

Dr. Shaw and the Squire had for many years been fast friends. The former had been in regular attendance upon the wife of the latter all through the illness which terminated in her death. He had also treated the squire on many occasions, securing the greatest confidence and warmest friendship. A word of introduction is due to the worthy gentleman, though in the Ards such is quite unnecessary. There quite a young man he took up his abode in Greyabbey. There he lived and there he died. He was a man utterly devoid of pride or ostentation; quiet, retiring, and unobtrusive. In manner and appearance he was modest and gentlemanly. He had charge of the Greyabbey dispensary, but in addition to that he enjoyed a considerable practice. With his patients, rich and poor, he was quite a favourite; in the esteem of the general public he stood high. The doctor never married. It was said that a lady, to whom he was engaged, lost her life by a melancholy accident at Bryansford and that the worthy man never recovered from the shock. Be that as it may, he remained a bachelor to the end of his days. His place of abode, which is still an object of interest in the village of Greyabbey, was a small and unpretentious house.

Here he dwelt alone, his sole attendant being a woman named Mary Nevin, who cooked his meals and kept his apartments tidy, and who, when her day's work was done, returned to her own house. The doctor was remarkably shy in company—particularly so with ladies. His figure was one well-known wherever he went, and he was easily distinguished at a considerable distance by the spectacles and the "Balmoral" cloak which he wore. As a physician he bore the reputation of possessing wonderful skill and a very extensive knowledge.

Such was the man into whose hands Squire Brown had fallen, and in no better hands could he have been. He was unremitting in his attention. The services of an experienced nurse had been secured, the doctor and she remained at the Big House day and night, and, assisted by Miss Brown, they kept constant watch over the sufferer.

Harry O'Neill seized an early opportunity of visiting Miss Brown, to offer his sympathy and his services, if he could be of any use. It was from him that she learned of Johnnie Hunter's arrest, and of the serious aspect of the case against him. Hunter had seen the solicitor retained by Harry O'Neill for his defence. "Tell me everything you know and I shall save you if possible," the attorney had said to Hunter. And Hunter declared his innocence; swore that he knew nothing of the robbery and attempted murder of the Squire, and yet he admitted having been at the house late that night; he admitted that the blood-stained ash plant was his property.

"What were you doing at the house," asked the attorney.

"I had business there," was the reply.

"With Squire Brown?"

"No."

"With whom, then?"

Hunter, shaking his head, answered—

"A wunnae tell that."

"My dear fellow, I am neither judge nor jury," said the lawyer, smiling; "I am not even a magistrate, but merely an ordinary attorney employed by your friend here to save your neck from—

ahem! to get you out of this little scrape. So you must tell me the name of the person you went to see, and also the nature of your business."

But the prisoner only shook his head.

"I'll tell you, sir," said Harry O'Neill; "he went as the bearer of a letter from me to Squire Brown's daughter."

Johnnie started to his feet. "Ye shudnae a tell't that, Harry," he exclaimed; "there's nae use in bringing either her name or your's intil it."

"Nonsense!" said O'Neill; "do you think that either Miss Brown or I would imperil the life or liberty of an innocent man."

"Diz she beleev A'm innocent?" asked Johnnie.

"What need is there for secrecy?" asked the attorney.

"I shall account to you for Johnnie's scruples," answered Harry. "I must tell you that I have been carrying on a correspondence with Miss Brown without her father's knowledge. Not wishing to trust the post lest my letters might fall into the Squire's hands I sent them by the hand of a trusty messenger. That messenger was your present client—Johnnie Hunter."

"Ha! a love affair," remarked the attorney; "But how do you account for the stick, Hunter?"

"A suppose A may as well oot wi' it a' noo," said Johnnie. "Weel, sir, A loast my stick that nicht, an' here's the wae it happened. Miss Brown was tae be watchin' at her wundey ivery nicht for me an' her letter. Her wundey was on the second storey; very weel, A made a split in the yin en' o' my stick tae pit the letter in, an' then by stannin' on the still o' the wundey unner hers a cud reach it up tae her."

The attorney nodded, and Johnnie proceeded—

"On the nicht that this affair happened A jest had laid my stick doon on the wundey still an' had my han' in my pokit tae get the letter whun a heerd a heavy fut cumin' roon the hoose. A thocht it micht mebbe be the Squire, an' so A run doon ower the saft gress an' hid among the laurels. The fut stappit; a keekit oot atween the bushes an' seen it wuz Black Ben. A think he had seen me, acause he stud watchin' for aboot twunty minits, an' whun he did gang oot o' sicht A had a noshin that he wuz aye watchin', an' so A slippit awa hame."

"Leaving your stick lying upon the windowsill," said the attorney.

"Yis, sur," replied Hunter.

"And that's all you know of this business, is it?"

"Afore God, sir, it is," said Johnnie, solemnly.

"Very well," said the lawyer, pocketing the memorandum book in which he had been taking notes, "we must make the best fight for you that we can. Then turning to Harry O'Neill, he added—

"I shall want your evidence, Mr. O'Neill, and you had better tell the young lady also that I shall require her as a witness."

"That will be unpleasant, but I suppose it will be necessary," said Harry.

"Absolutely necessary."

"We shall both be ready," said Harry.

And then the attorney and Harry retired, leaving poor young Hunter to brood in silence and alone upon the dreadful position in which he found himself placed.

CHAPTER XXVII

IN CONSULTATION

WHEN Harry O'Neill parted from the attorney and young Hunter he mounted his horse and galloped straight to Squire Brown's. As he approached the house he was observed by Annie, who met him at the door. Dismounting from his horse and handing the bridle to John M'Closkey, Harry entered the house and was conducted by Annie to her own sitting-room. Annie was delighted to see him, and anxious to hear of his interview with Hunter.

"Have you seen Johnnie?" she asked.

"Yes, Annie, I have."

"Well?"

"I am more than ever convinced of his innocence."

"Of course; no one suspects him," said Annie.

"The queer part of it all is that ash plant," replied O'Neill. "Johnnie admits it to be his."

"Does he?" asked Annie, in surprise.

"He does, Annie; he said he had split the end of it with his pocket knife; that when passing a letter to you he stuck it into the slit in the end of the stick, and, mounting upon a window sill he passed it up to you."

"And that is perfectly true," said Annie; "I remember having laughed at Johnnie's ingenuity."

"But, how did the stick become smeared with blood?" said Harry, "That's the puzzling point with me. Johnnie says that he was in the act of passing up your letter on that eventful night, when, hearing a step coming round the house he darted into the shrubbery, leaving his stick lying upon the window sill. There it remained, because not wishing to compromise you, Annie, and fearing that he was watched, he went home."

After a long pause, during which Annie was buried in deep thought, she looked up and said—

"Yes, Harry, I recollect waiting for your letter; I had been in bad spirits all day, and thought the gloaming would never come; at length I heard a footstep which I believed to be Johnnie's and had my hands upon the window to raise it when I heard the person, whoever it was, run away; then a heavier step approached and stopped. I waited until my patience was fairly exhausted, and then, concluding that you had not been able to write to me that day, I threw myself down on my bed and fell asleep. As you already know, I awoke hearing the screams of Jane that papa was murdered."

It was now Harry's turn to muse.

"Might not that step and the man who attacked your father be in some way connected?" he asked.

"Just what I was thinking," replied Annie.

"But do you know who the person was that coming upon Johnnie thus startled him?"

"No, Harry, I have no idea."

"It was *Black Ben*."

"Oh, Harry! could it be possible that he was the perpetrator of the deed?"

"I cannot tell, but I shall leave no stone unturned, Annie, to discover the culprit; as for poor, kind-hearted Johnnie Hunter, he is as innocent as the child unborn."

"I feel it, I know it," cried Annie; "and isn't it dreadful that he should be locked up in a common cell, branded as a robber and a murderer. Then look at his poor mother; I saw her to-day, Harry, and she is absolutely wild with grief."

"Poor woman!" murmured Harry.

"And isn't it strange, Harry, that she openly accuses Ben of being the guilty party, and endeavouring to attach the blame to Johnnie out of revenge."

IN CONSULTATION

"Revenge for what, Annie?"

"She would not tell me, but she said all would yet come right."

"And so it will, Annie; but there will be something very awkward and unpleasant for you and me in connection with Johnnie's trial. I have not yet told you of it."

"What is that?" she asked quickly.

"Under the greatest possible pressure from the attorney and myself Johnnie made the disclosure about his mode of conveying letters to you. The attorney says that you and I must both go into the witness box."

"Well, Harry, what matter, if by that means we help to establish Johnnie's innocence. Poor fellow! to think that he should have to suffer so much for us."

"Quite true, Annie, and I, for my part, am ready to make any and every sacrifice; but first look at the unpleasant position in which you will be placed. I wonder could it not be avoided."

Annie was silent for a few moments. Though unwilling to admit it, she did not like this new feature of the case and there was a shade of uneasiness upon her face. It brightened suddenly as she exclaimed—

"Harry, I shall consult Doctor Shaw; he is such a good, kind man, and his advice may be of much service."

"Do so, Annie, but remember there is no time to be lost. Johnnie will be brought before the magistrates on the day after to-morrow."

The lovers parted, and Annie, determined to lose no time, invited Doctor Shaw into her sitting room. There she disclosed to him all that Harry O'Neill had just told her, and she blushed and stammered not a little when making a frank avowal of the state of affairs between her and Harry, and of the manner in which young Hunter had been employed. "And now my dear, good doctor," she concluded, "I have come to you for advice, believing that your wise head can help me in this difficulty. Remember doctor, that I will not shrink from the exposure of my secret, however unpleasant that exposure may be, but some means may be devised whereby it may be avoided."

The worthy doctor, rising from his chair, paced up and down the room for fully ten minutes, buried in thought. At length, facing Miss Brown, he paused, and said—

"A good deal of mystery and doubt enshrouds this case. Could we but procure evidence of one witness, all that mystery and doubt would disappear, carrying with them that little difficulty of yours."

Annie looked up in his face eagerly.

"Who is that witness?" she asked.

"Your father," replied the doctor.

"Ah, doctor, is such a thing possible? Can it be that my father will recover?"

"It is quite within the bounds of possibility," replied the doctor; "I have, as you are aware, been giving this case my most careful study, and I think, nay, I am almost sure, that the performance of a certain operation, called trepanning, may restore to your father the use of his mental faculties."

"But the operation—is it dangerous?" asked Annie.

"By no means; at all events it is worth the risk. I meant, of course, to speak to you about this matter, and I may as well do so now. Listen to me attentively."

CHAPTER XXVIII

A STREAK OF LIGHT

SQUIRE BROWN'S daughter drew her chair close up to that which was occupied by Dr Shaw, and looking into his face attentively, waited for him to begin.

"Well now, Miss Brown," said that amiable gentleman, "I have, as you must be aware, been most attentive to your poor father since this sad event occurred. I have studied his case carefully, and have arrived at certain conclusions. As you will have noticed, your father, though seemingly unconscious, can swallow the food and medicine which we put into his mouth. The injuries sustained by him about the face are not of a serious nature and may soon heal. The same, however, cannot be said of the injuries to the skull. In one place, at least, a portion of the skull has been beaten in upon the brain. Now it is the pressure of such portion of the skull upon the brain which, in my opinion, causes your father's unconsciousness. Do you quite understand me?"

"Perfectly, Doctor."

"Well, then, if I am correct in my impression, we may take it for granted that, so long as the pressure on the brain continues, so long must unconsciousness continue."

"I see, doctor; and it is in connection with this, I presume, that you spoke of an operation," said Annie.

"Exactly," replied the doctor, "but I shall not attempt that operation until I have first held a consultation with some of my professional brethren, and, even should they agree with me, I must have your consent to it."

The doctor paused, and Annie sat in silence, buried in thought.

At length she spoke—

"You are hopeful of success, doctor?"

"Very hopeful, indeed," replied Dr. Shaw.

"And if you succeed—what then?" replied Annie.

"Why, then your father's consciousness will be restored, and, in the event of his ultimate recovery, he may live for many years in full possession of his senses."

The tears—but they were tears of joy—sprang into the fair girl's eyes as she clasped the doctor's hands and exclaimed—

"Oh, my dear Doctor, you have my full consent; let it be done at once, and may heaven grant the realization of your hopes and of my wishes!"

"The sooner it is attempted the better," said Dr. Shaw, "because, if we are successful, not only is your father restored to you, but the discovery of this would-be murderer follows."

"True! I had forgotten that," exclaimed Annie; "Oh, Doctor, there is not an hour to be lost. Surely justice demands that the experiment should be made."

"Depend upon it, I shall lose no time," said the Doctor, rising to his feet; "so now I must leave you for a time in order to procure the attendance here of Dr. Catherwood of Donaghadee and Dr. Whitla of Newtownards. You can see that my directions regarding the treatment of our patient are carried out during my absence."

"You may rely upon that," said Annie.

"There is another point," said the Doctor, turning round from the door which he had partly opened.

"What is that?" said Annie.

"Let what has passed between us just now be kept strictly secret; do not mention a single word of our conversation, or of our hopes, to any living soul. Bear this in mind, and hereafter you shall see the absolute necessity of this course."

The required promise was given by Annie, and half an hour

later found the worthy doctor being driven along, at a spanking pace, by the Squire's man, John M'Closkey. A few hours was sufficient for the Doctor to make his arrangements with the medical gentlemen who he had selected, and that being done he called at the Newtownards Bridewell to see Johnnie Hunter. He found the young fellow bearing up bravely; all his wants were being attended to; he stoutly maintained his innocence, and spoke hopefully of that innocence being established—how he did not know. The interview was a short one, but when Dr. Shaw left the prison there was a brighter look upon Hunter's face than had yet been seen since his incarceration.

As the Doctor walked down Regent Street he met the Sergeant of Police.

"Ah, Doctor, glad to see you," said that worthy, as he shook the doctor by the hand, "how is your patient, the Squire?"

"Not much improved," replied the Doctor; "it is a serious case."

"Any chance of his recovery, think you?" asked the Sergeant, anxiously.

The Doctor did not answer, and made as though to proceed upon his way. The Sergeant's quick eye noticed this.

"I trust, Doctor, I have not offended you," he said.

"Oh, no," answered the doctor, drily.

By this time the Doctor had resumed his course down the street, and the Sergeant had wheeled round and was walking by his side.

"The fact is, Doctor," said the Sergeant, "that I take a deep interest in this case."

"So do I," said the Doctor.

"There is, no doubt, much mystery about the case," the Sergeant went on; "the recovery of the Squire would at once solve that mystery."

The Doctor smiled. "Sergeant," he said, "our ideas upon this case appear to coincide wonderfully, but for certain reasons which it is not just now necessary for me to explain I have no wish to be seen in your company."

The Sergeant stopped, and looked hurt.

"You misunderstand me, I fear," said the doctor quickly, "where can I have a word privately?"

"The barracks would be the best place, I think," replied the Sergeant.

"Very well," said the Doctor, "I'll meet you there in half an hour."

So saying, the Doctor walked down towards Conway Square, while the Sergeant went off in a different direction.

Punctual to his appointment, Dr. Shaw presented himself at the police barracks. He found the sergeant at the door, waiting to receive him. "Follow me," said the Sergeant. The Doctor did so, and was conducted to the Sergeant's private room.

"Now," said the sergeant, as he handed the Doctor a seat, "we can talk here without fear of interruption."

"I would have written to you," began the Doctor, "but I noticed you felt hurt at a remark made by me to you in the street, and I therefore thought it better to seek for this interview in order that we might fully understand each other."

The Sergeant nodded.

"This affair at Squire Brown's," continued the Doctor, "is as you are aware, the all-absorbing theme of conversation. Now the public, as a rule, jump to conclusions with astonishing rapidity. Were you and I to be seen conversing together, it is difficult to say at what conclusion the worthy gossips might arrive, and, in the end, justice might be defeated."

The Sergeant looked puzzled. "I fail to comprehend you, Doctor," he said.

"Very likely," answered the Doctor, "but suppose you are following up a clue, you often find it necessary to keep the public in the dark."

"Certainly."

"Well now, we are agreed upon that," said the Doctor. "In this case your desire is to get hold of the guilty party?"

"No doubt of that, Doctor."

"Very well, it is my desire to assist you towards that object," said the Doctor, "but at present I must not disclose to you the nature of the assistance which I hope to be able to give you. Now, the attorney for Hunter's defence will apply for an adjournment when this case comes on. You will not object to that?"

"The magistrates who preside will very likely be guided by the reasons which Hunter's attorney may offer," replied the Sergeant.

"But, my dear sir," said the Doctor, smiling, "are not the magistrates guided pretty much by you and their Clerk? How would it be possible for them to get along without you? Why, man, you have more legal knowledge in your head than all our local luminaries put together."

The Sergeant smiled at the compliment paid him, and before the interview was over he had promised to comply with the doctor's wishes.

"And now," murmured the Doctor as he stepped towards Saunderson's in quest of his car, "now for the operation. Would that it were safely over."

CHAPTER XXIX

SAMMY TAMSON

THE Sergeant of the police had given orders that Johnnie Hunter should be treated with all due kindness and consideration. Consequently his friends were admitted at all reasonable hours, and the length of their stay was left pretty much to themselves.

Dr. Shaw had not long left Hunter when a welcome visitor was announced. It was William Taylor, the schoolmaster. Johnnie fairly caught him in his arms and almost squeezed his breath out.

"Johnnie, my boy, how are you?" cried the master, so soon as Johnnie would permit him to speak.

"There's naethin' wrang wi' me noo, mester, sae lang as you're here. Hoo's my ma?"

"Well, Johnnie, I need not tell you that she is sadly distressed on your account, but we do all we can to cheer her."

"That's richt, mester; keep up the buddy's heart, an' tell her A'll suin be hame tae pit in the corn. They micht a waited till we had the churn ower afore they brocht me here."

"I'm glad to find you in such excellent spirits, Johnnie," said Taylor.

"Agh, man dear, what wud mak me doon-hearted?" laughed Johnnie, "shair A wud stan twunty times mair nor this for the Squire's dochter an' Harry O'Neill. Whun did ye see Jeannie?"

"This morning, Johnnie; she sent you that," and Taylor slyly handed him a dainty note.

"God blis her!" exclaimed Johnnie, kissing the letter and putting it into his pocket.

"Read it, Johnnie, don't mind me," said Taylor.

"Na, man, A wull not," replied Johnnie, "as lang as you're here A'll no be lonely, an' when ye gang awa, what Jeannie sent me wull keep me frae thinking lang* A'll warrant ye."

Then the two friends talked of the coming trial, and of the probable result. Johnnie was confident of acquittal, and rattled away as though he had been at his own fireside.

"There are many things connected with the crime that are utterly beyond my comprehension," said Taylor; "for instance, where was Jane, the servant, and how did she not hear the noise caused by the fall of the Squire?"

"Oh, there's naethin' strange aboot that," replied Johnnie, "she micht be in some o' the oothouses, but mair likely she wuz oot coortin' wi' Sammy Tamson."

"Who is he?" asked the schoolmaster.

"A servant boy o' Tam Forgeyson's," answered Johnnie, "an' he's fair deein' aboot Sarah Jane, the Squire's lass."

"Is her name Sarah Jane?" queried Taylor.

"Ay, it is," responded Hunter; she maistly gets plain 'Jane,' but ye may be shair Sammy will gie her a' that she's entitled till hae."

As Johnnie said this he sat down upon the side of his bed, and putting his head between his hands burst into a fit of laughter, loud and long. The tears fairly ran down his cheeks, and when the fit was over, he wiped his eyes, looked up at the schoolmaster, and enquired—

"Did iver A tell ye aboot the trick that Wully Jamison an' me played on Sammy Tamson?"

"No, Johnnie, you never did," said the Master. "Some day when we get you out of this you can let me hear it."

"But what wull ye dae if they hang me?" asked Johnnie, laughing. "A'll jest tell ye it noo, mester, while its in my heid."

---

* 'thinking lang'—i.e., longing.

Taylor, glad to see Johnnie in such capital form, told him to proceed.

"Well, mester," began Johnnie, "ye mebbe dinnae ken Sammy, but ye micht a notised him that night at Corney's wake. It was him that et sae mony farls o' oaten breid an' sae much cheese. He's a great big awkward, shughlin kind o' fellow, but as saft an' as inocent as a wean. Some folks say there's 'a slate aff,' and ithers say that 'his week's up aboot Friday,' but a aye thought he was mair knave nor fule. He ansers Tam Forgeyson richtly, for he can gang through a slap o' work in yin day, but Mistress Forgeyson was aye compleenin' that he wuz a terble big eater. Puir fellow, mony a time a hae sut an' watched him at his males. He wud aye set his cher aboot a yerd aff the table, an' he would reach oot his big han', lift a farl o' breid, an' lay it on his knee. Weel, first he wud brek aff a wheen bits wi' yin han' an' pit them in his mooth; then he wud pit what wuz left on the tither knee, an' ivery noo an' then he wud reach forrit fur his bowl o' milk an' tak a drink. That wud a went on fur aboot half an hoor, an' he wud nether luk up nor speek a wurd a' the time. The Mistress wud a said till him—

"Well, Sam, A hope ye tuk yer fill," an' he wud say back till her—

"Oh, weel, A hae tuk a 'pit ower' at ony rate."

"Weel, Mistress Forgeyson begood tae notis that there wuz odd times he didnae eat near sae muckle as he did for ordinar, so she kep' her e'e aboot her, an' what dae ye think but yin day whin she wuz up on the barn laft lukin' for eggs, she fun' a wee box somthin' like what ye'll see in grocer shaps for keepin' Mertindale's blackenin' in, an' my deers, wuzn't this fu' o' breid an' butter an' caul meet. Well, she saw Sam cummin aff the laft the same efternoon, an' notised him drawin' his sleeves a wheen times across his mooth an' thinks she, 'my boy, yer no daein' that fur naethin.' Weel, she watched her appartunity till gang back till the laft, an' behold ye but the blackenin' box wuz gie an' near empty. Mistress Forgeyson tell't me this in a great saykret, an' sez she—

"My, whaur diz he get it onywae?"

"In yer ain cubberd, Mistress Forgeyson," sez I.

"Na, he diz not get it there," sez she, "for the breid's bakit wi' anither soart o' flooer nor a use a'thegither, an' it's no my butter ether."

"Diz he gang oot at nichts?" sez I.

"He diz that," sez she, "an' gie an' affen he's no back whun Tam an' me gangs till oor bed."

"Noo, lave it till me," sez I, "an' if we dinnae fin' oot whaur the breid an' beef cums frae it'll be a queer thing."

"Well, A turned the thing ower an' ower in my min', an' furst A thought A wud lie ahint a dyke and watch for Sam gaun oot, but efter that A made up my min' till speak till Wully Jamison, so that nicht A had a lang crack wi' him aboot it. My, but he did lauch, an' sez he—

"A think A ken whaur he gets the meat."

"Dae ye?" sez I, "whaur is it?"

"Shair he's coortin, Sarah Jane, the Squire's servint lass, an' that's whaur he gets it," sez Wully.

"A wudnae say but yer richt," sez I.

"Heth, A'm purty shair o' it," sez Wully, "hooaniver," sez he, "we'll very suin fin' that oot."

"What wae?" sez I.

"We'll watch whaur he gangs at nicht," sez Wully.

"Weel, we let Tam Forgeyson intil the saykret. Tam said he wud gie us a signal whun Sammy gied oot for a nicht's coortin'."

"Ay, but hoo will ye ken?" sez I.

"Oh," sez he, "he aye weshes his face an' pits a big muffler roon his neck."

"An' what wae wull ye let us ken?" sez Wully. Tam scratcht his heid and studied a bit. Then he luckit up an' lauched, an' sez he—

"Ye ken the soon o' my auld gun whun she gangs aff."

"Man, A dae that," sez Wully. "A wud ken the crack o' yer Queen Anne the wurl ower."

"Well," sez Tam, "the first nicht A see Sammy makin' fur gaun oot, A'll tak doon the gun an' say that A'm feered she's gettin' dirty, an' that A had better cleen her oot."

"Good!" sez Wully, "A see it my boy."

"Weel, then," sez Tam, "A'll danner roon till the back o' the hoose an' let her aff. As suin as ye hear the shot, slip doon through the lang meadow an' lie doon aback o' the whundyke aside Jamey Blizzard's loanin' till ye see Sam gaun bye, an' efter that," sez he, "A maun leev the thing in yer ain han's."

"A cud harly get a wurd oot o' Wully that nicht gaun hame, he wuz that deep in thocht, an' ivery noo an' then he wud stap on the road an' lauch ower ocht.

"What's tikellin' ye, Wully?" sez I, but he made me nae anser.

"Twa nichts efter that Wully and me wuz gettin' reddy till gang till a singin' class whun we heerd Tam Forgeyson's gun gaun aff.

"Thonner!" sez Wully, an' he whuppit up his hat an' stick.

"It wuznae lang till him an' me wuz at the hidin' place, and we wurnae got weel laid doon till Sammy went past talkin' till himself, but we cudnae hear what he wuz sayin'. We let him get a guid peece aheid o' us, an' then Wully an' me slippit alang keepin' on the tither side o' the dyke till we cum as near the Squire's as we thought was safe, an' then we laid oursels doon an' keekit through the hedge. We cudnae a been in a better place, an' it wuz a mercy we went nae farder, fur Sammy stappit an' luckit roon him a bit, an' then gied a wee whussel. Weel he whusseled ether twa or three times, and then Wully whuspered till me—

"A see a lass cumin' doon the back pad."

"Wully had sherper e'en nor me, an' it was two or three minits afore A cud see her, an' forbye it wuz a kin' o' duskis. Wully gied me anither dunch, an' sez he—

"Ay, indeed, an' as shair as A'm here but it's Sarah Jane; lie quate fur yer life."

"It wuznae lang till Sam and her met, an' the twa o' them cum dannerin' up the loanin' and passed close by us. A heerd Sarah Jane sayin'—

"There's yin o' the kye wuz amaist chockit the nicht on a piece o' a turnip, an' A hae tae stae wi' her a while o' the nicht, an' help Johnnie M'Closkey till gie her warm drinks, so A'll no can stae oot lang."

"Bad luck till her!" says Sam.

"Oh, Sam! ye shudnae say that," sez the lass, "fur Spotty's the best coo in the byre."

"Well, bad luck tae the turnip, then!" sez Sam.

"Sarah Jane lauched. Then A heerd her sayin'—

"Well, Sam, A maun bid ye guid nicht."

"A lay shakin' till my sides wuz sare tryin' till keep in the lauchin'. Sam had a kin o' stappage in his speech, and forbye that he could niver soon' the letter 's,' and whun ocht vexed him he grew far waur at the talkin'. Whun the lass bid him guid nicht A heers him sayin'—

"Oh, o—o—dang thay's it, Thay—Thay—Tharah Jane, ye'll no lave me that thoo—thoo—thoon?"

"Indeed, indeed, a cannae help it Sam, but a'll see ye nixt Monday nicht," sez she.

"Wull it be at the th—th—thame plaith?" sez he.

"Better till gang for a walk at the whunnynowes,"[*] sez she, "whaur we'll no be disturbit. A wud rether bring ye intil the hoose, but the mistress wudnae aloo it."

---

[*] i.e., whinny knowes—whin (gorse) covered hillocks.

"Mair th—th—thame fur her," sez Sam. "A'm thair thee coo—coo—coortit yinth herthel."

"A cudnae get slippin' ocht oot for ye the nicht," sez the lass.

"Oh, A hae iver thae muckle ye—ye—yit," sez he, "o' the l—l—latht ye gied me."

"Did ye no like it?" sez she.

"Ay, wuman, A did," sez he; "A niver did t-t-taitht ocht thay nithe," sez he, "an' whun A gang back the nicht A'll gang up till the l-l-laft an' finith it."

"Wully nippit me till A gied A jump. "Wheesht!" sez he, "slip up alang the dyke as quate as iver ye can efter me," and on he went twa dooble till we wur oot o' heerin' an' sicht, and then he streecht himself up and tuk till the runnin'.

"What ir ye up till?" sez I.

"A want till be at the hoose ten or fifteen minutes afore Sam," sez he, "an' if A dinnae pit a dose in his breid an' butter that'll mak him wunner what's wrang wi' him, my name's no Wully Jamison."

"We wur baith clean oot o' breth whun we got till Tam Forgeyson's. Wully liftit the latch, an' whun we went in Tam an' the wife wur sittin' at the fire.

"Did ye see him?" sez Tam.

"A did, man," sez Wully, "an' it's a' richt; hae ye ony Kyann pepper in the hoose, Mistress Forgeyson?"

"Na, Wully, a hae not," sez she, "what's wrang?"

"No very muckle," says Wully, "but A want A taste o' somethin' hot."

"Wud mustard dae?" sez Tam.

"No very muckle," says Wully, "but be quick aboot it. A hae a wee snuff o' rid pepper in my pocket, an' A'll mix a' thegither."

"Here ye ir," sez the mistress, handin' doon a half pun' tin canister o' musterd.

"Noo, stae whaur ye ir, ivery yin o' ye, till A cum back," sez

Wully, an' oot he went, takin' the musterd wi' him.

"What's wrang wi' the boy, onywae?" sez Mistress Forgeyson.

"A lauched, an' says I—

"I think A ken what he's efter; hooaniver A'll let him tell ye himsel'."

"Wully wuz back in twa or three minutes an' he handed Tam the canister. Tam keekit intil it, an' sez he—"Heth boy, ye haenae left very muckle."

"Well, we a' sut doon, an' Wully tell't us he had laid the mustard an' rid pepper gie an' thick atween the pieces o' breid an' butter, an' left the box sittin' wi' the lid up an' then he gied us a' the instructions what we wur till say an' dae whun Sammy cummed in.

"But hoo wul ye ken whuther he haes et the breid or no?" sez I.

"Oh, it'll no be hard till know that," sez Wully, "tak' my wurd fur it his mooth wull be gie an' warm, an' he'll be inquirin' efter a drink o' water A daur say."

"Pit the water can oot o' the road," sez Tam; an' his mistress run awa an' set it oot o' sicht.

Jest wi' that we heerd a fut gaun by the door.

"That's Sammy," sez Tam.

"Whaur's he gaun?" sez I.

"He's awa till the laft till finish his breid an' butter," sez Wully.

In aboot ten minits Sam cum in an' tuk a sate at the fire. He hadnae richt sut doon till he riz up an' tuk aff his muffler, an' A notised him pittin' it till his mooth an' koughn. Then he sut doon again.

"That's a brave nicht ootside," sez Wully.

"Y-y-yithur," sez Sam.

"A thocht A heerd yer fit gaun by the daur a wheen minits ago," sez the mistress.

"Oh ay," sez he. "A wuth doon at the byre l-lukin' wuth the kye fothered."

Then he riz agen an' tuk a noggin doon aff the dresser, an' we heerd him fumelin aboot whaur the water can sut. Tam throwed a lump o' fir on the fire, an' it lichtit up the hoose, till ye cud a seen tae pick up pins an' needles.

"Wur ye wantin' ocht?" sez Mistress Forgeyson.

"Ay, A wud like a moothful o' cauld water," sez Sam, "but a doot there'th nane in," an' wi' that he put up the noggin an' sut doon agen. The crater, A heerd him sughin' ower ocht, an' he wud aye draw the back o' his han' across his mooth and wipe his e'en wi' the sleeve o' his weskit.

Tam Forgeyson spauk oot then, an' sez he—

"By-the-bye, Mary, wuz it you laid the puzhin fur the rats?"

"Whauraboots?" sez she.

"On the barn laft," sez Tam.

"Na, Tam," sez she, "A laid nae puzhin."

"Weel," sez he, "A wuz up on the laft wi' Wully Jamison here, an' we cum on some breid an' butter in a box an' we cudnae think o' ocht else that it wud be fur, an' Wully heppened tae hae wi' him a pickle o' sumthin' that they use doon in the Squire's for killin' rats, so we slippit a grane o' it atween the slices, an' left the box wi' the lid apen."

A wuz watchin' Sam wi' the tail o' my e'e, an' A cud see him gettin' as rid as a coal, an' then as white as a sheet.

Wully lauched, an' sez he—

"Tak my wurd fur it, Mistress Forgeyson, if ony o' the rats eat their supper aff yon they'll no bother ye agen in a hurry."

Sammy drawed his han' across his stumak, an' then wipit his face wi' his weskit sleeve.

"My, but puzhin's a queer thing," sez I. "Hoo lang wud it tak it till kill a buddy?"

"Oh, this sort taks a guid while," sez Wully, "an' the rayson it's considered sae muckle better nor ither puzhins is that whun the rats eat it they leev a lang time, an' the tithers ir sa scaured wi' their sufferins that they cleen lea the place an' niver cum back."

Puir Sammy, his mooth wuz gapin wide open, but we tuk nae notis o' him.

"The deer man!" sez Tam Forgeyson, "an' hoo diz it affect them?"

"It burns them maist dreedfully," sez Wully; "an' they wud gang mad if they did nae get a drink o' water."

Sammy spauk oot at last, an' sez he—

"Miththreth Forgethyon, for the l—l—luv o' God gie me A moothfu' o' water?"

"A wull, Sammy, dear," sez she; an' awa she run, fur a seen she thocht a peety o' the crater, an' she brocht him a noggin' o' water.

Wully gied the fire a poke wi' the tangs, an' sez he, jest as the drink wuz bein' reached till Sammy—

"But the keruyus pert o' it is, Tam, that if they drink water it taks fire like gunpowder, an' blaws them intil a thoosan peeces."

"The dear thave uth!" sez Sammy, an' wi' that he pitched doon his hale lenth in the flair.

We a' gethered roon him, an' that made him waur. He rowled ower an' ower, an' if Wully hadnae gruppit his heid he wud a knockit his brains oot on the hearthstane.

"What in the wurl's wrang wi' ye?" sez Tam.

"Th—th—then fur the doctor," sez Sammy, "A'm puzhined."

"My, shockin'!" sez the mistress, "wha puzhined ye, waen?"

"A et what wuz in th—th—the blackuin bozth," sez he; "O, Thara Jane, what wull A dae?"

"Wully, dear, what's to be din?" sez Mistress Forgeyson.

"Bring the dokter f—f—fatht an' thenn fur the meinither," sez Sammy, "fur my inthide's a' in a bleethe."

"Lift him intil bed," sez Wully.

"Guid's blithin' be on ye," sez Sammy, as we carried him till his bed, an' the crayter, the hale road he was sabbin like a waen an' moanin'.

"Oh, Tharah Jane, Tharah Jane."

Whun he wuz in bed, Wully turned roon till Mistress Forgeyson, an' sez he—

"Hae ye ony castor oil in the hoose?"

"Na, no a taste," sez she.

"Well, bring me the saut box," sez Wully.

Mistress Forgeyson brocht the saut box an' Wully run till the spoon box fur a spoon, an' liftin' it fu' o' saut.

"Noo, Sammy, my man," sez he, "sup this up."

Sammy tuk it that greedy that he near swalleyed spoon an' a'.

"Fetch me sum buttermilk," sez Wully.

The mistress brocht nearly a canfu' an' a noggin tae lift it wi'. Weel, hoo muckle o' that buttermilk Wully made the crayter swalla, A dae not ken, an' efter that he rubbed him a' ower wi' his han's. A declare ye wud a thocht he wuz a rael dokter.

"Hoo dae ye feel noo, Sammy?" sez I.

"A'm gettin' better," sez he. Of course so he wuz, an' afore bedtime he wuz a' richt."

Johnnie, having completed his story, went into another fit of laughter.

"You are a rare lot of boys in your district," said the schoolmaster; "I shouldn't like to quarrel with any of you."

Here they were interrupted by the entrance of the Sergeant, who wished to speak to Hunter, and the schoolmaster, having promised to deliver sundry messages for Johnnie, took his departure.

CHAPTER XXX

SUSPENSE

THE day following that treated in the last chapter was an anxious one with the Squire's daughter. The preceding night, indeed, had been a sleepless one. Hope and fear alternately filled her breast. The success of the proposed surgical operation would bring back life to her father, and direct the sword of justice in its fall; its failure would deepen the gloom of the cloud which now enveloped her, and bring uncounted misfortunes upon her and her friends.

The hour of noon found the three doctors at the Big House. While Annie kept her own room, her heart throbbing with painful anxiety, the medical men, intent upon the business in view, stood around the bed of the unfortunate Squire. Doctor Shaw, with the greatest deliberation, stated his opinion; a minute diagnosis followed, and that opinion was endorsed by Doctors Catherwood and Whitla. Then the necessary preparations were made, the door was locked, and the operation began. In those days, surgery was not what it is to-day; even the appliances were inferior to those now in use, and critical operations were not nearly so often undertaken as they are now. The life of Squire Brown hung in the balance, but he was in the hands of skilful practitioners. Let the curtain be drawn upon the scene which was being enacted in his chamber.

Wearily, oh, how wearily, passed the time with Annie Brown. Now she stood waiting for a message from the doctor, and anon she would sink upon her knees, praying, with clasped hands and tearful eyes, for the deliverance of her father. Suddenly she started. Was that a step approaching the door? Yes, it was! She had not strength, so wildly throbbed her heart, to approach or open it. There was a tap, and Annie in a faint, choking voice, said "Come in." Dr. Shaw entered. He did not need to speak; his face told all he could have said. The operation had been successfully accomplished.

With an exclamation of joy Annie fairly flung herself into Dr. Shaw's arms, and that worthy man seemed to feel his position even more keenly than the scene which he had just left. Where ladies were concerned Doctor Shaw was remarkably shy, and in the present instance he had literally not a word to say, as the fair girl showered upon him tears, blessings and questions. At length he seated her upon the sofa, and sat down by her side. Then he strove to allay her feverish anxiety.

"Everything has turned out as I expected and as I wished," said the doctor; "your father has spoken, he is now conscious, and unless something unforeseen should happen, his life is saved."

Annie was completely overcome with joy. There and then she would fain have rushed to her father's apartment had not the Doctor restrained her and assured her that his patient must be kept perfectly quiet, and that he must not be disturbed at present. "I shall remain here," he added, "and as soon as I judge it safe you shall see your father."

Then he left her and joined his colleagues downstairs.

Meanwhile how fared it with Johnnie Hunter, a prisoner in his lonely cell, charged with a crime the penalty of which might be life-long transportation? He had been before the magistrates and a crowded court; but the proceedings were as brief as they were formal. Poor Johnnie failed to comprehend what was passing, and ere he had begun to fully realise his position, he was taken back to his cell.

What had passed was this; the charge had been stated and an adjournment asked for to enable evidence of an important kind to be produced. This was granted, but the magistrates refused to accept bail for Hunter, considering the very grave nature of the charge. This was a sad blow to Johnnie's mother. The good woman was in court, and such was her grief of beholding her son led away in custody, that some kind friends were obliged to remove her from the court-house.

During the next fortnight Squire Brown's neighbours were in a perfect fever of excitement. It was observed that the sergeant of police made frequent visits to the Big House; the solicitor in charge of the case had been there twice, remaining each time for more than an hour. All this the neighbours had seen, but they had been unable to do more than guess at the object of these visits. Even Jane, the Squire's servant, with all her cleverness, failed to learn anything of what was going on. And so time passed.

♦♦♦♦♦♦♦♦♦♦

It is a court day. From an early hour the people of Newtownards could not fail to observe an unusual number of well-dressed farmers wending their way towards the court-house, prepared to wait and be jostled and crushed in the hope of securing a place in the Seat of Justice. "This is the day o' Johnnie Hunter's trial," went from mouth to mouth, and when the hour for the opening of the court had arrived, an immense crowd had collected in that vicinity. A rush followed the opening of the doors, and in a very few minutes the building was literally packed with an excited throng.

"Silence!" cried a burly policeman, as the dignitaries of the bench entered and took their seats. Then a hush fell upon the vast crowd, while every eye and every ear were strained to see and hear what was about to follow. Drs. Shaw, Whitla, and Catherwood, together with the solicitor retained for the defence, sat at the solicitor's table. Hunter was at the side of his attorney, and as he surveyed the sea of eager faces, he now and then nodded to such friends as he recognised.

Hunter's case was called, and the Sergeant stepped into the box. He deposed to the facts which had come to his knowledge in the usual stereotyped, police fashion. He told how that from information received he had gone to Squire Brown's residence. He described what he had seen there, and then proceeded to relate the circumstances connected with the arrest of the prisoner. He concluded by stating that the chief witness for the prosecution was the Squire's bailiff, upon whose sworn information Hunter had been arrested.

"Produce him," said the presiding magistrate.

"Ben Hanlon!"

As that name, shouted at the top of the sergeant's voice, rang through the building, there was a murmur among the occupants of the Court-house, so loud and so prolonged that the cry of "Silence!" was repeated several times by the policeman to whom that duty was entrusted. A movement in the crowd, at the rere of one of the passages, indicated the whereabouts of Black Ben, and that worthy, after a good deal of pushing and jostling, reached the witness-box. As the bailiff stood up in the box a hush fell upon the audience, and for a moment the stillness of death prevailed. Then, painfully distinct and clear, came the tones of the Clerk, who, as he placed the Sacred Volume in Ben's hands, said—

"The evidence which you shall give in this case shall be the truth, the whole truth and nothing but the truth, so help you God—kiss the Book."

Ben kissed the Book, cast a furtive glance round the court, and, in obedience to the Sergeant, sat down.

Then the Sergeant proceeded to question him.

"You are agent or bailiff for Squire Brown?"

"Yis, sur."

"How long have you filled that position?"

"Weel, A shud say close on ten yeer."

"You remember the night of the robbery at the Squire's?"

"A dae."

"Tell their Worships what you saw that night."

"Well, yer honors," said Ben, turning to the Bench, "A had been in the byre at yin o' the kye that wuz poorly, an' as A cummed roon by the en' o' the hoose A heerd a fit runnin' awa an' seen a man jumpin' in amang the laurel bushes."

"Did you recognise that man?" resumed the Sergeant.

"Eh?"

"Did you know that man?"

"A did."

"Who was it?"

"It was young Johnnie Hunter."

"Do you now see the same person in court?"

"A dae; that's him sittin' there." (Points to the prisoner.)

"What did you do then?"

"Naethin'."

"Didn't you remain there for some time watching Hunter?"

"A did."

"Did he come out from his hiding-place?"

"Na; A seen nae mair o' him that nicht."

"Do you recognise that stick?" (Here the sergeant produced and handed to Ben the ash plant found in the Squire's room.)

"A dae."

"Tell their Worships what you know about it."

"A seen Johnnie Hunter cuttin' that stick in the plantin' a wheen days afore the robbery. A tuk it oot o' his han' at the time an' lukit at it. That's hoo A ken it."

"When did you next see that stick?"

"When you shewed me it."

"That was the day after the robbery?"

"Ay."

"And you swear to that stick as the identical one you saw Hunter cutting shortly previous to the robbery?"

"A dae."

The Sergeant then explained to the magistrates how he had found the stick, and that Hunter, after being arrested, admitted it to be his. He had no further evidence to produce, save that of the medical gentlemen, who would describe the nature of the injuries to the Squire.

"Does anyone appear for the prisoner?" asked the Bench.

"I do," said Hunter's attorney, and as he rose to his feet a flutter of excitement passed over the crowd in court.

"May it please your Worships," continued the attorney, "I appear for the prisoner Hunter, and I claim the medical gentlemen as my witnesses. With regard to this man, Hanlon, better known as 'Black Ben,' I do not propose to put any questions to him at the present juncture, but I reserve the right to cross-examine him a little, should I think it necessary." Then turning to the Sergeant, he said—

"Sergeant, accommodate your witness with a seat, and see that he does not leave the court. I may require him shortly."

CHAPTER XXXI

A SURPRISE IN COURT

THE human countenance, if natural, is expressive. Most faces do indicate feeling or passion. Even the most stupid features or those most trained and disciplined to conceal this natural language, speak betimes in the most unmistakable manner.

Ben Hanlon's face was a hard one. The greater portion of it was concealed by his coarse and matted beard. It was not a speaking face, nor an intelligent one by any means, though cunning strongly marked it. And yet, with all, a sudden change overspread it—a shadow as of terror—when Johnnie Hunter's attorney, with a meaning look at the police Sergeant, said—

"Sergeant, accommodate your witness with a seat, and see that he does not leave the court. I may require him shortly."

Yes, it did not require much skill in physiognomy to see that Black Ben felt uncomfortable under the keen glance of the lawyer. He evidently wished himself well out of the prosecution, and as far as possible from the Newtownards Court-house.

As the police officer led Ben to a seat where he could have him constantly within view, there was another of those audible murmurs which now and then, like a breeze of wind, pass over an excited auditory, and cannot be repressed.

There was once more a cry of "Silence!" from the burly policeman, and, as the solicitor for the defence began to address the court, the stillness was such as would be observed in a house of public worship.

"May it please your Worships (he said), I appear here to-day on behalf of the accused, John Hunter, and rarely have I entered upon the defence of a prisoner with such a willingness or with such confidence of success. I was first attracted towards this case by the air of mystery which surrounded it. At the close of an autumn day, in a quiet and peaceable district of County Down, a gentleman farmer is attacked in his own sitting room, brutally beaten, and left for dead, and then, as is assumed, the culprit or culprits decamp, carrying off the contents of a cash box. And this outrage, too, is perpetrated upon a quiet and unoffending man, who lived at peace with all his neighbours. He was indeed, almost a recluse, living entirely within doors; leaving the management of his property to the witness who has just left the box, and the control of his household affairs to his only child—a young lady now in court, and who is a favourite with all her father's tenantry. The police were at once communicated with, and your good Sergeant here, with characteristic promptitude, was soon upon the scene of the outrage. He it was who discovered the empty cash box, and the loose documents and papers; and, when his attention was drawn to this ash plant, stained and smeared with blood, he naturally concluded that the ruffian who sought to beat out Squire Brown's brains had used this stick as his weapon, and had, unguardedly, left it behind him. That there was a robbery committed I have no doubt. That the thief also meant to be a murderer I am equally certain. The wounds inflicted upon Squire Brown's face and head were of a truly dreadful nature, and the wonder is that there is still breath in the poor gentleman's body. By the mercy of Providence two well-known medical practitioners chanced to be passing just when the Squire's condition had been discovered by the inmates of the house, and these gentlemen—Dr. Whitla, of this town, and Dr. Shaw, of Greyabbey, dressed his wounds. These doctors are in court, and will, when called upon, describe the nature and extent of the injuries inflicted.

"And now, your Worships, I have said that I am convinced there was a robbery and a deliberate attempt to commit murder.

A SURPRISE IN COURT

Well, I am equally confident, nay more so, that my client, John Hunter is entirely innocent of the horrible charge preferred against him. (Applause in court.) What is the case against him? He was seen in the neighbourhood of the house upon the night in question. Who saw him? Ben Hanlon. A stick is found in Squire Brown's, smeared with blood, and that stick is identified as having been cut in the Squire's plantation by my client some days previous to this affair. Who identifies it? Ben Hanlon. That's all the evidence against young Hunter. I have here a copy of the information sworn by Hanlon, and upon which Hunter was arrested. This kind-hearted bailiff goes further in that than he did in the witness-box. In this document he alleges that the prisoner was anxious to procure money in order that he might be in a position to ask the hand of a certain young lady, and that one day, in a public house in this town, he overheard my client say, "I'll raise the money if I should rob the Squire for it." We admit the ownership of the stick, and we do not say that the words quoted by Hanlon, or their equivalent, may not have been used. But we shall, I think, be able to show that Hunter lost that stick outside the Squire's house, and as for the expression 'I'll raise the money if I should rob the Squire for it,' I think it is easy of explanation. There are certain phrases used by all classes of people that, taken in a certain light, and connected with certain occurrences, would seem remarkable, but which taken in their ordinary sense have no more meaning than the simplest exclamation employed to denote surprise, anger, or admiration. Now, in the district where this most unfortunate occurrence took place, Squire Brown was the leading resident, and when my client used the words complained of—that is if he did employ them—he simply meant that he was determined to procure money, however great the difficulty might be, but that he intended the words to have their literal meaning no one who knows John Hunter, would for a single moment believe. (Applause in court.) While I am confident that the evidence which I can produce will clearly and satisfactorily establish the innocence of my client, I cannot refrain from thus dwelling upon the features of this remarkable case. I admit that the grounds of suspicion fully warranted the arrest of Hunter, but he shall not suffer upon that account. On the other hand, the improbabilities of his guilt are so striking that all who are familiar with the district, the circumstances, and with the character of my client, were naturally surprised beyond measure at what they considered a gross outrage upon justice. My client is the only son of respectable parents; the sole support of a widowed mother. From his very boyhood he has worked for the support of that mother. His temper and disposition are of the most mild and winning kind, and of all others John Hunter would, I am confident, be the last man to embrue his hands in the blood of a fellow being."

The attorney sat down for a moment at the conclusion of his speech (of which the above is but a brief outline, culled from the newspapers of the period), and, as he resumed his seat, the long pent-up feelings of the spectators found vent in a perfect thunder of applause. In vain the magistrates frowned and gesticulated; in vain the stout policeman roared "Silence!" until his face seemed bursting; the hearts of the people had been touched by a master hand, and they must, in the way best understood by them, pour out a tribute of admiration.

Silence was shortly restored. Doctor Shaw took his stand in the witness box, and having duly sworn, described in medical phraseology the injuries which Squire Brown had sustained.

The attorney handed Dr. Shaw the ash plant, and then asked—

"Would a stick, such as that, inflict wounds of the character you have described."

"It might."

A SURPRISE IN COURT

"The Squire was for a considerable time in a comatose or insensible condition?"

"He was."

"You suggested a surgical operation?"

"I did."

"What was the nature of it?"

"Trepanning; as I stated before, a portion of the skull was pressing upon the brain causing insensibility."

"I understand; well, Doctor, has that operation been performed."

"It has; I was assisted by Dr. Whitla and Dr. Catherwood."

"Successfully?"

"Very."

"And you hope for favourable results?"

"Yes, the most favourable."

"Thank you, Dr. Shaw; you may go down."

"Have you any other witnesses?" enquired the Bench.

"I have," answered the attorney. "Doctor Whitla is here and Doctor Catherwood; they can, if necessary, corroborate Doctor Shaw as to the nature of the Squire's injuries."

"Quite unnecessary," said the presiding justice, turning to his colleagues, who looked wise, and nodded assent. Then, addressing the lawyer, he asked—

"Is that all?"

"No, your Worship, I shall now call my chief witness—Squire Brown!"

Had a thunderbolt exploded in that crowded building, greater consternation could not have prevailed. The occupants of the body of the court, gallery, and passages, sat or stood spellbound, while the jolly-faced, burly policeman—whose duty it was to call for the witnesses—stood with gaping mouth from which there issued no sound. But the lawyer and his client, the medical gentlemen and Harry O'Neill smiled quietly as though they rather enjoyed the astonished aspect of the Court. At length the lawyer, turning to the Sergeant, with a knowing look at that mystified individual, said—

"Have the goodness to call my witness."

The spell was broken, and as the name—

"SQUIRE BROWN!"

rang through the court and was repeated outside, a commotion was observed near the entrance. The crowd made way, and there, sure enough, pale, thin, and haggard, supported on each side by the arm of a friend, was Squire Brown, slowly approaching the witness box, at a moment when everyone—save the few entrusted with the secret of his recovery—felt certain that he was upon the very confines of another world.

CHAPTER XXXII

THE REAL CRIMINAL

THE most intense excitement prevailed as Squire Brown was assisted into the witness box. Every eye was fixed upon him; every ear was strained to catch the first words that might fall from his lips. At length the unexpected witness was comfortably seated in the box, and then the silence was broken by the clerk, who, in his accustomed slow and measured tones, administered the oath—

"Your evidence in this case shall be the truth, the whole truth, and nothing but the truth, so help you God. Kiss the Book."

Then the attorney rose to his feet, with a look of triumph in his eyes, and commenced the examination of his witness.

"You are called Squire Brown?"

"I am." The answer was given in a low, feeble voice, yet it was quite audible.

"You remember the night upon which the attack was made upon you at your house?"

"I do."

"You recollect all that transpired on the night prior to the infliction of the blows which rendered you unconscious?"

"Perfectly."

"You are still weak in body from the effect of those blows?"

"I am, indeed."

"But you are in possession of sound sense and judgment?"

"Yes, thank God; my mind is perfectly clear and collected."

"Well now, Squire, their Worships will patiently bear with you, I am sure, considering the state of your health. Be good enough to describe what occurred upon the night of which we speak."

The Squire gently inclined his head in token of assent, sat for a few moments silent, and then said—

"I remember all. I had previously had an interview with several of my tenants who complained of the manner in which they were treated by my bailiff, Ben Hanlon. Some of them alleged that he was defrauding them by claiming rent which had already been paid, and they all expressed their determination to pay their rent in future either to myself or to my daughter. They urged upon me to have a careful examination made of Hanlon's rent-books, in order to satisfy myself as to how their respective accounts stood, and this I promised to do. When they had left me I sent for Hanlon. Without saying anything to him about the deputation or the object of their visit, I asked him to bring to me all his books, as I wished to take a run through them to see how the accounts stood with my tenants. He went away, and returned shortly, bringing the books with him. I desired him to leave these with me, and to be in waiting in the kitchen, so that he might be at hand in the event of my wishing his assistance. I spent several hours—I can't say how many—in going through the books, and I discovered sufficient to satisfy me that what the tenants had stated was only too true. They had been defrauded and so had I. While still occupied with my investigations a tap came upon my door, and in response to my 'Come in,' Ben Hanlon entered. He remarked that it was getting late, and enquired if he might go. 'Come here, Hanlon,' I said, 'I want some explanations from you.' He closed the door and came to the table at which I was sitting. I pointed out to him that a great many of the blocks, or counterfoils, had been torn out of the rent receipt book, that in numerous instances the figures entered in counterfoils differed from those upon the receipts which my tenants had left with me for inspection and I failed to find entries in the cash book for the sums—half-yearly gales of rent—one paid by widow Hunter, the other by a man called Brown. Hanlon did not appear at all disturbed. He quietly remarked that he would look into the matter on the following day and satisfy me that everything was right. 'You must do it now,' I said, 'for if I should sit here all night I shall have this affair investigated.' I then questioned him regarding the various items about which I had my suspicions. His answers were hesitating and extremely unsatisfactory. At length I lost my temper, and starting to my feet I said—'Hanlon, you are prevaricating. I entrusted all these things to you and you have betrayed your trust. But you shall not escape unpunished, for I shall have you transported. Hanlon, you are a ruffian and a thief!'"

Here the Squire paused, as if overcome by the recollections which crowded upon his mind. One of the magistrates, with kindly thoughtfulness, handed a glass of water from the bench to Dr. Shaw, who was standing at the witness box beside his patient. The Doctor passed the water to the Squire, who sipped a little of it, gave back the glass and then proceeded—

"Hanlon called me a liar. I ordered him from the room. He lifted his stick, as I thought to retire, but suddenly faced me, and raising the stick suddenly, struck me on the head. I remember nothing more."

As the Squire ceased speaking the crowd stirred, and a murmur was heard like the first sound of the rising storm.

The attorney who had been all the time standing, then said—"Do you see Hanlon in Court?"

The Squire had evidently seen Black Ben from where he sat, for he turned deliberately round, and pointing towards the bailiff said—

"There he is."

"And you swear that Ben Hanlon, your own bailiff, was the person who committed the crime for which my client, John Hunter, was arrested."

"I do—."

The Squire added some other words, but they were drowned in the ringing cheer that burst from an auditory now stirred beyond control. No attempt was made to suppress that wild outburst of delight, and for a brief space the din was absolutely deafening. Squire Brown was assisted to descend from the witness box and to take a seat at the solicitor's table. But the novel proceedings were not yet at an end, and very soon the crowded court again became silent to witness the next act in this singular drama. All eyes were now strained to catch a glimpse of Black Ben, who sat cowering in his seat with the Sergeant of Police uncomfortably near to him. The next moment, upon the order of the Bench, John Hunter was free, and Black Ben was a prisoner. No sooner had the welcome announcement been made to Johnnie that he was a free man, and might leave the Court without a stain on his character, than that worthy seemed determined to leave the precincts of the Court for the purer air outside. It was no easy matter to push through that solid mass of human beings, for there was now a general movement towards the door, and the people poured out into the streets, where stood a crowd of these who had been unable to gain admission. The news spread from lip to lip with lightning-like rapidity, and the scenes which followed have never had a parallel in Newtownards. Many persons are still alive who took part in that day's proceedings, and who have detailed them to the writer of this story. Johnnie Hunter was surrounded by an eager and excited throng of people, all anxious to congratulate him upon his release. Then a few sturdy fellows caught him up, raised him upon their shoulders, and, followed by a cheering crowd, carried him in triumph through the streets. A like ovation awaited the attorney when he made his appearance in the street. Next came Squire Brown. The "covered car," in which he had been brought to town, stood waiting at the Courthouse door. The moment

THE REAL CRIMINAL

he had taken his seat in the vehicle, a number of his sturdy tenantry unyoked the horse, and seizing the shafts, drew the conveyance after them for fully a mile.

And what of Ben the bailiff? He feared to face the angry crowd which he knew awaited him out of doors, and begged of the Police Sergeant to allow him to remain in court as long as possible. The Sergeant deemed it advisable to yield to the request, and Ben was kept for several hours in the caretaker's apartments. In the evening, when the crowds had dispersed, he was led forth, handcuffed and surrounded by a strong guard, who marched him off to be confined, pending his trial, in Downpatrick jail.

CHAPTER XXXIII

RETRIBUTION

FEW persons, if any, were surprised at the result of the memorable proceedings in the Newtownards Courthouse on the day of Johnnie Hunter's trial. Johnnie's mother had all along spoken out boldly, accusing Black Ben of the crime, and her opinion was also held by nearly everyone in the neighbourhood, but then there was no evidence against him, however strong suspicion might be. The storm of indignation against Ben was great when it became known that Squire Brown, snatched from the very jaws of death, had told the story of the crime. Had Hanlon fallen into the hands of his neighbours that day, the legal tribunals of the land would not have been further troubled with him.

In his lonely cell sits Ben, the bailiff. No visitors trouble him; there are no loving messages from the outer world for the unfortunate wretch; he is left to his fate and to the bitter reflections which are swelling in his blackened heart.

Several days had passed, and Ben's agony of mind was beyond endurance. Shut out from the world, his plans all destroyed, his life blasted, what was there now to live for? A thousand times he had cursed himself and the fate which impelled him to commit his crime. He had heard of prisoners escaping from jails. What if he could escape! But a brief inspection of his cell with its thick stone walls and iron-barred window convinced him of his utter hopelessness. Then he sought to win over the turnkey who brought him his meals; as well might he have talked to stone.

About a week had elapsed when one day Ben heard footsteps approaching and the sound of voices engaged in conversation. The steps paused at the door of his cell; a key was thrust into the lock and turned; the door was pushed open, and a visitor entered. It was the Rev. David Parke.

The reader may here be informed that Ben had been a most devout member of Mr. Parke's congregation. He was regular in his attendance, paid his stipend promptly and willingly, and was, in the eyes of his pastor, a most exemplary man. The kind-hearted clergyman was overwhelmed with grief and astonishment when the tidings of Ben's arrest and imprisonment were communicated to him, and he would at once have started off to commune with him had not business of pressing importance detained him. Now that he stood in Ben's cell a single glance convinced him that he was in the presence of a guilty man, and that his visit was unwelcome to the culprit.

Ben was seated upon his bed. He looked up as Mr. Parke entered, then dropped his face into his hands, resting his elbows upon his knees.

Mr. Parke was the first to speak. "Ben I am truly grieved to see you here," he said, gently and kindly.

The unhappy man made no reply.

"I came, as is my duty," the minister went on, "to see if in any way I could serve you."

Still no answer.

"Come, Ben, look up at me and speak to me."

This time Ben looked up and answered—"A wud rether no a seen ye."

"In that you are wrong, Ben," said the minister; "it is my duty to visit you. I have not come here to rebuke you or say anything which would add to your unhappiness. You are friendless, Ben, at least so you have often told me, and if you have any little commissions to be executed, entrust them to me; if you have anything to communicate, anything to say which would lighten the load at your heart, I am here, Ben, your minister and spiritual adviser, willing to serve you in any way I can."

Ben had again covered up his face, and relapsed into sullen silence. Suddenly he looked up and asked—

"What'll they dae on me?"

"Who?"

"The law."

"If found guilty, Ben, you may be transported for life."

"God preserve me!" groaned the wretched man. "They'll fin' me guilty, sir; hoo cud A contradict the Squire?"

"Then you admit your guilt, Ben?"

"There's nae use in denyin' it, sir."

"Poor fellow! What could have induced you to commit such a crime?"

"A never meent tae dae it, sir, A niver did indeed; but yin step gars ye tak anither. A may niver see ye again, an' A feel disposed tae tell yer reverence the hale story. A had A grudge at twa or three o' the tenants an' A thocht that by makin' them appear ahint wi' their rents A cud bring 'injekshins' agen them and turn them oot o' their farms. It wuz easy enuch din, but A niver spent the money an' that pert o' the thing can be set richt."

"But what ill-feeling could you have entertained towards Widow Hunter, a woman whom every other person liked?" asked Mr. Parke.

"Ay, an' A likit her tae; a likit her ower weel; it wuz that made me dae as A din tae her."

"I don't understand you, Ben."

"A wanted her for a wife, yer reverence, but she wudnae hae ocht tae say till me, an' so A swore tae hae revenge, but A niver kent it wud end this wae. A wudnae a struck the Squire if he had nae a spauk sae sherp till me. The first blow felled him; my bluid wuz up, an' A battered him then on the heid an' face, till A wuz shair he wuz deid. The servant lass wuz oot for the evenin', and the young mistress wuz in her ain room, so that naebuddy heerd what wuz gaun on. A went oot an' trevilled richt roon the

RETRIBUTION

hoose tae luk if A could see onybuddy aboot. It was then that A seen young Hunter runnin' doun amang the laurels. A stud watchin' till he went awa' an' as a wuz gaun on roon till the backdoor A seen an ashplant lyin' on yin o' the wundey sills. A liftid it an' lukit at it, an' kent it in a minit. It wuz Johnnie Hunter's an' he maun hae left it there by mistak. The divil put a thocht in my heid then that akwelly made me lauch. A cud pit suspicion on Hunter, get my revenge, an' save mysel'! A tuk the stick intil the Squire's room an' drawed it a wheen times through the bluid that was on the floor; then A left it there. Ye ken the rest."

"Did you take any money?" asked Mr. Parke, who had listened with evident pain to Ben's confession.

"A did."

"Where is it?"

"Wi' a' the rest. Tell them tae lift the hearthstane in the kitchen an' they'll get plenty. They can dae as they like wi' it noo."

"Ben, I am sorely grieved at all this," said the minister; and then he urged the self-confessed criminal to seek comfort and forgiveness from an offended Deity. But it was casting seed upon stony ground. Ben maintained a stolid silence until the clergyman, feeling that for the present his words were of no avail, rose to depart.

When he had left, Ben rose and paced his narrow cell, with knit brows and gloomy face. "Transport me for life!" he muttered over and over again. "Transport me for life! Na, they'll nivir dae that."

The shades of evening were gathering upon the Jail Hill, and the darkening shadows were stealing in through the grated windows of the narrow cells as their miserable occupants prepared to retire to their comfortless beds. A turnkey, on his usual rounds, drew the small door slides and peeped into the cells of which he was in charge. Some of the prisoners were asleep, dreaming, perhaps, of freedom; others tossed restlessly about as though sleep had forsaken their eyelids. When he reached Ben Hanlon's cell and looked in he started back, and his face turned ghastly white. Then he called to another turnkey to come to him.

"Something wrong here, Bill," he muttered, as he thrust his key into the lock and then pushed open the door. No wonder the two men stood speechless and appalled. In a corner of the cell, suspended by a leather belt from a pipe which crossed the ceiling, hung the still warm but lifeless body of BLACK BEN!

The wretched man died by his own hand and the prophecy of poor old Corney O'Neill when he said "*That man wull niver dee in his bed*," had been fulfilled.

CHAPTER XXXIV

CHRISTMAS EVE

TIME had passed. It was Christmas eve. In the cosy little room where we first made the acquaintance of Squire Brown, sat that worthy man and his daughter. Annie was sewing, the Squire was reading, both operations being conducted in silence.

The Squire had changed very much since our first acquaintance with him. He was paler; his hair was turning white; his face had not yet regained the hue of robust health. But he was less of a recluse than formerly. He went out almost daily amongst his tenantry, for they had touched his heart by their devotion to him during his life-trial. It was not unusual to see him climbing over a ditch and walking side by side with some tenant who was ploughing, or sitting by the fireside of some other, chatting pleasantly upon the topics of the day.

Towards his daughter, too, his manner had undergone a change. Pettishness and moroseness had entirely disappeared. He showed more affection for his child, was more communicative, and made more frequent enquiries after her wants than formerly.

And what of Annie? The close observer might have read traces of care upon her young, fair face. Some silent sorrow at her heart was surely placing its mark there.

The Squire's eyes wandering now and then from his book. It failed to interest him or else his thoughts were elsewhere. At length he spoke—

"Well, Annie, is everything ready for to-morrow?"

"Yes, papa, everything."

"Annie," resumed the Squire, with a tinge of sadness in his voice, "it was upon a Christmas day that your dear mother last sat at table with me in this very room. Ever since her death my Christmas dinners have passed quietly indeed. You have been my only companion at the meal; and now that I look back, I cannot but feel how dull you must have felt your companionship."

"Oh, no, papa; I never felt it dull."

"It was but natural, my child, that you should," answered the Squire. "However, Annie, I desire change, both for your sake and my own. To-morrow we shall have a guest for dinner."

"Who can it be, papa?" asked Annie, quickly.

"Harry O'Neill," replied the Squire, very calmly and quietly, and he dropped his eyes upon his book, so that he might not add to his daughter's confusion by noting the warm flush that spread over her face and neck.

There was no response from Annie, and the Squire, rightly interpreting her feelings and her desire to be left alone, rose to his feet.

"I am tired, Annie, and shall go to bed."

"Very well, papa," was the reply, as Annie, glad of an excuse for rising, went to fetch the Squire's candle.

"Good night, dear," said the Squire, kissing his daughter, and adding as he left the room—"Don't sit up too late, my girl."

He was gone, and Annie was alone. Poor girl, how great was her bewilderment. She stood, for several minutes, gazing straight before her, but seeing nothing. Seeing nothing! I am wrong. She gazed into empty space, but she beheld there, as she did wherever she might turn her eyes, the bold, handsome face of Harry O'Neill. Flinging herself into the easy chair just vacated by her father she covered her face in her hands. By-and-by tears of silent joy ran slowly through her fingers. Let us not intrude upon her reveries.

CHAPTER XXXV

CHRISTMAS DAY

CHRISTMAS morning dawned crisp, and bright and bracing. Scarcely had the first rays of the winter sun chased away the darkness of the preceding night than sights and sounds upon all hands indicated the birth of the national holiday. There was no gun tax in those days. All classes of men and boys could carry gun or pistol and walk about in quest of "a shot" without the slightest dread of meeting a spying excise officer, who, with an impudent display of petty authority, would demand, "Shew me yer lisens!" What a time there had been, for several nights before this Christmas day, cleaning up the old "Queen Anne" guns, pouring boiling water down their barrels, and pumping away with the iron ramrod, round which was tied a handful of tow, until the water ran clear from the touch-hole.

The day gave promise of glorious sport, and the country population was astir betimes. Here and there, in a grass field, amid shouts of laughter such as can proceed only from the lungs of sturdy country youths, the game of "shinney"[*] was in full swing. Merry was the work and heavy were the blows which rang off the old tin can, or other object used as a "bool."[†] Others, with cautious mien and noiseless tread, stole from point to point, eagerly scanning every bush which might be giving shelter to a hare. Boys carried horse pistols, and pistols made from every conceivable form of tube, bellows' pipes, teapot "stroops," and tin whistles being the most common. The very dogs knew it was Christmas day, and barked and capered about in wildest glee.

---

[*] i.e., shinty.
[†] i.e., a ball.

In a field at the rere of Widow Hunter's small holding a merry party had assembled for the purpose of shooting at "whites" for a goose. This has ever been a popular sport in the neighbourhood, and it is a harmless game. One end of a flat piece of wood is planted firmly in the earth, and a piece of paper called a "white" is stuck against the face of the board about five feet from the ground. The contestants shoot at the "white," and he who can plant in it the largest number of pickles of shot carried off the prize.

The party in question numbered about a dozen, and included Mr. Taylor, the schoolmaster, Johnnie Hunter, Sam M'Givern, Wully Yeaman, Johnny M'Closkey, and Davey Morrow, a carpenter of Ballyboley, who had no equal at making a coffin or "stocking" a gun.

"Noo, boys, it's time ye wur at it," shouted the worthy Sam, as he stepped up to the post, "wait an' A'll pit up a white fur ye."

As he spoke he drew from his pocket a cold potato, removed part of the skin, spat upon the denuded portion, and rubbed it briskly upon that part of the wood to which the paper was to be attached. Next he dived one hand after another into his various pockets. His search was evidently a vain one, for he shouted—

"Haes ony yin a piece o' paper, for dang saze the bit A hae got."

The schoolmaster produced a copybook, which he had fetched with him to enter the score in. Tearing out a leaf, he handed it to Sam, who declared—

"Hide-an-hare! The very thing, but it's a shame tae waste the guid paper."

The men began to load. It was a tedious process, and those who were engaged in it little dreamt of the days of elegant breechloaders, when a double-barrelled gun would have both barrels charged ere the rusty ramrod of a Queen Anne could be withdrawn from its fastenings. Johnnie M'Closkey was known

CHRISTMAS DAY

as a dead shot. Many a time has the writer of this story, when a boy, accompanied him, and beheld, with a feeling of awe, how unerring was his aim. Let us watch M'Closkey while he "charges." He raises the hammer and examines the flint. Then turning the muzzle of the piece to his mouth, he blows into it, in order to satisfy himself that the passage contains no obstruction. The hammer is then let down, and, drawing a horn from his pocket, he empties a quantity—sufficient nowadays for several shots—of powder into his broad palm, holding the cork of the horn in his teeth. He empties the powder into the barrel, re-corks the horn and returns it to his pocket, and pulling a quantity of coarse tow from another receptacle, stops it into the muzzle of the gun and drives it home with the iron ramrod. Next he produces a lemonade bottle, half filled with shot, and spilling out a couple of ounces at least, he slily spits on it, sends it after the powder and follows it with more tow. The saliva was supposed to serve the purpose that wire does in the present day—that of holding the shot together after its discharge from the gun. Then there was the priming process, and M'Closkey was ready to toe the line.

"Hoo mony shots?" he asked.

"Threes apiece," answered Hunter, "an' we'll draw cuts for wha's first."

By this time all were ready. The schoolmaster plucked a dozen blades of grass, and, trimming them all of different lengths, arranged them between his finger and thumb. The drawing decided the order of shooting. M'Givern having drawn the longest blade, was to shoot first. There were only six guns in the party, so that borrowing and lending was necessary. Sam borrowed Davy Morrow's.

"Diz she kick, Davey?" he asked.

"She diz, man, like the very deevil!" was the assuring reply.

"Teer me up, but A think A can haud her!" cried Sam, cheerily, as he stepped to the line and eyed the "white."

"Noo, boys," he went on, "watch me gettin' the giss (goose) jist at the first shot."

So saying, he deftly raised the ponderous weapon, placed the butt against his shoulder, and glanced along the barrel. A minute of breathless stillness followed: then there was a flash and a roar so terrific that the farmyard fowl screamed with terror, and even the pigs uttered unearthly yells. Sam was gently rubbing his shoulder as the schoolmaster stepped up to the post to ascertain the result of the shot.

"Hoo many piles?" cried several.

"One!" laughed the schoolmaster, as he jotted down the score in his copybook.

"Jean Tate an' Matty Wuds!" yelled Sam, as he thumped the butt-end of his gun upon the ground and then returned it to Morrow.

"A'm feered ye'll no get the giss, Sam," remarked Morrow, with a laugh.

"She kicks like bleezes!" said Sam in a sulk, "A'm shair A had the 'white' cuvered when A pu'd the trigger."

Thus the sport proceeded, the match lasting for upwards of three hours. Johnnie M'Closkey was declared the winner, and that worthy, stepping over to a hedge which skirted one side of the field, drew forth from a thorn bush, where he had concealed it, a bottle of whiskey, and treated the company. There was neither cup nor glass amongst them, so each man followed his neighbour and sucked from the bottle. But what of that! The liquor was good, and every man could take just so much as he relished.

As M'Closkey tucked up the goose under his arm, M'Givern, with a loud laugh, asked the party had they heard what he had said to a temperance lecturer in Greyabbey the night before.

"No, Sam, let us hear it," said the schoolmaster.

"Weel," said Sam, "the buddy had talkit for a lang time aboot

CHRISTMAS DAY

the herm it diz ye tae drink whuskey, and whun he wuz aboot finishin' up, sez he—'Oh, my friens, wud that A had the wings o' a burd, that A micht flee ower the hale country, and talk aboot temperance.' A cud stan' it nae langer, an' A cried oot frae the daur whaur A wuz stannin'—Hoots man! Afore ye flee'd a mile ye'd be shot for a giss."

A shout of laughter followed Sam's story, and the party dispersed with keen appetites for their Christmas dinner.

CHAPTER XXXVI

LOVE'S REWARD

LONG ere that Christmas morning dawned, the Squire's daughter had left her couch and was busily engaged with her household duties. How she did wonder under what circumstances her father and Harry had met. Why had Harry not written to her about this. Perhaps she would receive a letter from him this morning! And then, how she watched the old eight-day clock, and thought it surely must have stopped, the hands moved so slowly! Would Crackenfudge never arrive? Every five minutes did Annie look from the window for the letter-carrier's approach, and at last she was rewarded by a sight of the woman coming towards the house. There was an open door and a warm welcome for Crackenfudge as she handed the young lady several letters, exclaiming, at the same time—

"A merry Christmas tae ye, mem."

"I wish you the same," was the cordial response; "come to the kitchen and warm yourself."

Having so said, Annie bounded upstairs, for she had recognised Harry's hand-writing upon one of the letters. Let us follow her to her room, where, gaining admittance ere she hastily bolts the door, we can peep over her shoulder and read the contents of the eagerly looked for communication.

"Newtownards, 24th Dec., 18—.

My Darling,—Such news as I have for you! My heart's throbbings render my hand so unsteady that I can scarcely hold my pen. I met your father yesterday in Regent Street. Our eyes met and somehow I could not withdraw mine. What was my surprise to see him smile! But that was not all. He stopped when he had reached me, and, holding out his hand, caught mine in a cordial grasp. 'Harry,' he said, 'I am truly pleased to meet you. I have been wishing to see you, and would have written to you had I known your address. The last time we met I spoke unkindly to you—rudely, indeed. But I did not know then what a fine, noble fellow you were and I now apologise. Can you forgive me, O'Neill?'

I tell you, Annie, I felt like one in a dream. What answer I made I cannot tell, but I stammered out some sort of a reply. He said more, and wound up by asking me to spend Christmas Day at the Big House if I had no other engagement! What is there on earth could keep me from joyfully accepting an invitation so unlooked for? And so I shall be with you to-morrow, and my heart tells that all will be well. Our soul's desire may be nearer attainment than either of us imagines. I can write no more. May this Christmas be a joyous one indeed, for both of us, is the prayer of your ever devoted

HARRY."

Again and again did Annie read those precious lines. Then, carefully folding up the letter, she concealed it in her bosom, and with flushed cheeks and quickly throbbing heart went downstairs to look after the preparation of breakfast. The meal passed, like most others, in comparative silence, the Squire paying more attention to his newspaper than to his breakfast, and Annie was glad of this, because she could not trust herself to engage in conversation, and to eat she found impossible.

Harry O'Neill arrived at twelve o'clock, and was warmly received by the Squire. Annie's reception of her lover was such as she might have extended to a casual acquaintance, but Harry understood the silent language of the hand and eye.

Fashionable hours did not prevail at the Squire's. He dined at one. The meal was substantial, and, for a country squire's table, sumptuous. Never before had Annie seen her father in such capital spirits. He laughed and chatted with Harry, who soon felt himself quite at home and a privileged guest.

Shortly after dinner was over, the Squire, during the absence of his daughter, addressing Harry, said—

"Come upstairs with me for a few minutes; I wish to have a talk with you."

Rising as he spoke, he left the dining-room and went upstairs, followed by Harry, who wondered what the end of all this would be.

"Now," said the Squire, when he saw Harry seated and had ensconced himself in a capacious easy chair, "I have got something to say, and the sooner I have it off my mind the better. You remember our last interview in this house?"

"I do, Squire."

"I have already apologised to you for my rudeness upon that occasion, and now tell me, do you entertain the same feelings for my daughter now that you did then?"

"I do!"

"Then you are free to wed her, O'Neill. She is very dear to me, and I am naturally anxious that she should marry wisely and well. I have heard from Dr. Shaw of your untiring devotion to her interests and mine, when I lay between life and death. He told me all that you did, and I am convinced that you are a manly, honourable fellow. You called yourself a 'Son of the Sod.' It is to your credit that you were humbly born. You have brains, my boy, and a true heart. These are but seldom associated with high lineage and what the world calls blue blood. Harry, my daughter is yours. May you both be happy."

Harry sprang to his feet, and, grasping the Squire's hand in both of his, stammered forth his thanks, scarce knowing what he said.

"Well, well, my boy, prove yourself worthy of her; she is a good girl." Then, after an awkward pause, he added—

"By the way, you are fond of skating and so is Annie. There is splendid ice upon the big dam. Suppose you and Annie go for an hour's skating before tea, and while I write some letters."

Nothing could have pleased Harry better. Ten minutes later the happy couple were on their way to the ice, talking of—— need I say what?

♦ ♦ ♦ ♦ ♦ ♦ ♦ ♦ ♦ ♦

"Ma!" shouted Johnnie Hunter, dashing into his mother's cottage at a pace which thoroughly scared the good woman, and endangered the lives of a flock of hens which she was feeding on the kitchen floor—

"Ma! what'll A tell ye?"

"Guid save us, dear, what's wrang?" asked the widow, with a look of alarm, and setting down her wooden dish of oatmeal and potatoes upon the dresser.

"Shair Harry O'Neill an' Miss Broon's oot skatin' on the big dam!" he gasped.

"Haud yer tongue!" cried the widow; "my guidness, if her da catches them he'll tak' her life."

"Deil a fear o' him!" exclaimed Johnnie, "shair they're gaun tae be merried."

"Blethers an' balderdash!" said Mrs. Hunter; "it's makin' fun ye ir."

"May A niver stir, ma, but it's the God's truth! Harry tell't me himsel'. He tuk his denner at the Squire's the day an' it's a' settled. We're no tae gang tae bed the nicht till Harry comes, an' he'll tell us the hale story."

The widow stood like one thunderstruck. The news was as welcome as it was unexpected, and she was quite overcome by it. With a sweep or two of her extended apron and a vigorous "whesh!" she drove out the hens, closed the half-door, and sat down in her wooden armchair.

"Yer shair A'm no dreamin', Johnnie," at last she said.

"Na, wuman, yer far frae it," laughed Johnnie.

"What aboot the denner, ma? A'm jest stervin' wi hunger, so A em."

"It'll be ready in a minit, dear," she replied; "A didnae ken whun ye wud be in or A micht a haen it sittin' on the table. Waen dear, but ye hae put me that throo ither A dinnae ken what A'm dain."

Then she rose and drew the little round deal table near to the fire, and spread upon it a coarse but snow-white cloth, and in a very few minutes the meal was laid. A plate of mealy, smiling potatoes; a piece of nice boiled bacon, with a dish of "curleys;" a duck, stuffed with meal, potatoes, and onions, and roasted in an iron pot upon the turf fire; plenty of oat-cake, butter and milk, constituted a seasonable and appetising meal.

"The smell o' that's eneuch tae bring back the deid," said Johnnie, as he drew his chair towards the table, and attacked the roast duck something after the fashion of the famous Andy Straiten.

"A thocht A wud a haen the giss hame fur ye," he continued, "but Johnnie M'Closkey wuz ower money fur me. He jist put in twa piles mair nor me. That auld gun o' Gordan's is nae use; she went aff wi' me yince jist as A put my finger on the trigger."

Thus Johnnie rattled away, and as he did so the duck and its accompaniments were rapidly disappearing. At length he stopped eating, put down his knife and fork, and heaved a long sigh.

"Ir ye din, dear?" asked his mother.

"A'm sorry tae say A em," was the answer.

"Did ye eat till ye wur fu'?"

"A did, ma; A'm like what the lass at the Carrowdore suree said—A'm jest as fu' as a dug!"

"For shame, Johnnie!"

"Well, A declare, ma, it's the truth; ye cud tuch it wi' yer finger!"

"Johnnie, ye hae nae menners ava," said the widow, smiling. Johnnie sat for some minutes silent. Then suddenly looking up, he shouted—

"Ma!"

"Weel, dear?"

"Cum here an' sit doon; a want tae talk till ye."

Mrs. Hunter sat down by the fire and began to knit.

"What hae ye got tae tell me?" she asked.

"Harry O'Neill's gaun to be married."

"Ye tell't me that afore," said the widow.

"An' so am I," said Johnnie.

The widow dropped her knitting, and looking at her son, with open mouth and eyes, exclaimed—

"A doot ye hae been takin' sumthin' stronger nor water whun ye wur oot."

"Ay, A had a hauf yin; but A'm tellin' ye the God's truth, ma. Harry an' me made a bargain lang ago that whun he got merried to his lass A wuz tae get tied tae my yin."

"An' wha's yours?"

"Jeannie Banks, o' coorse!" said the young fellow, in a tone which implied that everybody should be aware of the fact.

"Weel, dear, A hope it'll be for yer guid, but A think yer baith far ower young."

"No yin bit, ma! ye cudnae dae a guid thing ower suin. It'll no' be lang till ye'll hear o' us bein' awa' at Mister Macauley's gettin' the leeshins."

The widow made no answer.

"It'll be a big day, ma."

"What day, Johnnie?"

"The day o' the dooble waddin'. It'll be a petty o' the whun dykes, A can tell ye, an' we'll hae a dance sumthin' like a dance.

Hoots! the punch ball at Dorrey's Hill wull be naethin' till't."

Seeing that his mother did not enter into the spirit of his arrangements, Johnnie rose from his seat, whistled to his dog, and, accompanied by it, struck off across the fields in search of sport.

CHAPTER XXXVII

A DOUBLE WEDDING

BALLYGILBERT Presbyterian Church has always been a favourite place for the celebration of marriages. It occupies a retired and pleasant site upon the county road leading from Belfast to Bangor, about a couple of miles distant from the latter town.

At the period of which I write, the Rev. John Quartz, a native of County Down, had just been ordained to the ministry and installed at Ballygilbert. Never did pastor and people become more rapidly knit together in the bonds of Christian affection and love. Gifted with a richly cultured mind, an eloquent delivery, a pleasing and prepossessing presence, the young minister rapidly acquired immense popularity. Wherever he preached crowded congregations listened with breathless attention to the chaste language, the glowing poetic imagery, and the burning eloquence which distinguished him as a preacher; wherever he visited, old and young received him with every manifestation of pleasure, regarding him not only as their affectionate spiritual teacher but also as their true earthly friend and adviser. After the lapse of so many years, no higher testimony could be borne towards the worthiness of both shepherd and flock than this—they are still united! Many and tempting, no doubt, were the offers of gold and position made to the distinguished preacher to wile him away to the great cities and their luxuriant tabernacles. But he refused them all, remaining true to his first choice and happy in the retirement of his rural home amongst the Sons of the Sod to whom he ministered.

Squire Brown was an ardent admirer of Mr. Quartz. Struck by an address which he heard him deliver at a congregational soiree in the church of which he was a member, the worthy Squire soon made his way to Ballygilbert, where he rented a pew, and, despite the distance, was quite a frequent hearer. As a matter of course, the popular clergyman was often a guest at Squire Brown's, and it is not to be wondered at that Annie expressed a wish to have her marriage ceremony performed by Mr. Quartz, and in his own church.

One morning in the month of February which succeeded the Christmas of which I have been writing there was an unusual amount of stir and bustle in the vicinity of Ballygilbert Church. People were seen approaching it from both directions, some on foot, some on horseback, others on cars and vehicles of various descriptions. It was the day when Harry O'Neill was to be joined in wedlock to the Squire's fair daughter, and when the handsome Jeannie Banks, "for better, for worse," was to wed our rollicking friend, the widow's son. The circumstances connected with the double event and with parties interested therein were sufficient to excite more than ordinary interest, and consequently the turnout of people to greet the happy couples was the largest ever witnessed in that neighbourhood.

The weather was extremely mild; signs of Spring were visible on the hedgerows and upon the trees; the roadway was pleasantly dry, and the sun shone with cheerful brilliancy.

The clergyman was the first of the actors in the pleasing life drama to appear upon the scene. His progress was of necessity slow. There were so many people with whom to shake hands and say a pleasant word, that hurry was out of the question. And, as he passed along, many a kind word and complimentary phrase must have reached his ears, such as—

"Ay, ye may weel say that!"

"Whaur wud ye see the likes o' him?"

"There's naething stuck-up or prood there."

"A doot we'll no' can keep him lang."

A DOUBLE WEDDING

"A wonner wull he be gettin' the words said himsel' some o' these days."

"There's a guid wheen o' the lasses lukin' at him onywae." &c., &c.

A shout in the distance caused all to look in the direction from whence it came. Several handsome carriages, each drawn by a couple of magnificent white horses, came dashing along at rattling pace. Instantly a cheer was raised, and then a rush was made for the church. Capacious as the building is, it proved too small on that occasion, and many were unable to obtain admission. Every pew and every inch of standing ground, pulpit and pulpit stairs included, were occupied, to the no small inconvenience of the bridal parties.

The utmost good order prevailed, and not even a whisper was heard as the minister commenced the ceremony. It is needless to describe the happy looks of the bridegrooms, the blushes of the brides, the little acts of awkwardness, inseparable from such occasions, or the kisses and congratulations at the close. Suffice it to say that all passed off smoothly and pleasantly, and that when the service was over, the building was emptied more rapidly than it had been filled.

It was no easy matter for the married couples and their companions to reach their carriages. There was an amount of crushing to get a glimpse of the brides that had to be put up with good-naturedly, Johnnie Hunter came in for the lion's share of attention, and some of the salutations which greeted him elicited roars of laughter from the crowd. Pressing close to the bridal party were many of Johnnie's neighbours and acquaintances. Old Dominie Harvey, with beaming face, was there; Donegall Charley, Fitty M'Cormick, Davey Morrow, Sam M'Givern, Johnnie M'Closkey, Sam Stewart, Tom Gaw, Tom Brown, Davey Henry, Whulty Regan, Tam Dowlan, Davey Askin, Robin Byers, Wully Yeaman, John Gibson,

Gummery Patton, and a host of others were there, cheering, shouting, and wishing all sorts of good luck, but above all the din could be heard the shouts of the Ballyboley Hoogher, and Sam M'Givern's voice as he now and then exclaimed—"Life in London! this is fun." "Teer me up, but they're fixed noo!"

At last the carriages were reached and the parties took their seats. The word "Belfast" was given, and away they dashed, followed by showers of rice, old shoes, and slippers, and a cheer such as has rarely been heard so near the sacred precincts of a church.

We shall not follow the gay company. Having breakfast at a fashionable restaurant, Mr. and Mrs. O'Neill started for Dublin and Killarney, while in the evening Mr. and Mrs. Hunter—in deference to the wishes of the lady—sailed for Scotland to spend the honeymoon in the "Land o' cakes."

Before saying adieu to our friends, whose doings we have been attempting to chronicle, let us attend the soiree and ball given at Dorrey's Hill on their return.

CHAPTER XXXVIII

DORREY'S HILL

OUR story opened with a merrymaking in the old barn at Dorrey's Hill, and the closing scenes take us back to the self-same building.

Squire Brown, having learned that steps were being taken to get up a grand demonstration on the return of the lately wedded couples, sought an interview with Taylor, the schoolmaster (who had filled the post of "groomsman" at Johnnie Hunter's wedding) and authorised him to say that he would defray the entire cost. This was welcome news to the committee, and they at once set to work. The chief difficulty was to procure a room sufficiently large for the accommodation of all who would expect invitations. No schoolhouse in the neighbourhood would have held half the number who would turn out, and, of course, to have the entertainment in a place of worship would have been out of the question. Teugh M'Kay solved the difficulty.

"Tak' it tae Dorrey's Hill," said he.

"The very place," cried several.

"Too far away," said the schoolmaster.

"No yin bit," was the response, "it'll stretch oor legs an' gie sum o' us jist the mair time tae see the lasses hame."

And so it was settled, and thus, in the early part of March, exactly fourteen months from the night of the famous Punch Ball given in aid of Corney O'Neill, the old barn was the scene of a memorable entertainment given in honour of Corney's son, Johnnie Hunter and their wives.

What a wonderful change of circumstances! And what a transformation had even the old barn undergone. The rough walls and still rougher roofing were completely hidden by masses of ivy and evergreens spread by skilful hands and plentifully besprinkled with flowers—natural and artificial. Tam M'Connell, the Carrowdore nailer, had good reason to remember the occasion. Home manufacture was encouraged in those days, and Tam had a full week's work hammering out nails upon his old anvil for the decoration, and manufacturing hooks from which to suspend some fifty or sixty oil lamps willingly lent for the night. Numerous appropriate mottoes, the handiwork of the schoolgirls of the district, served to relieve the monotony of the floral decorations.

Tea was laid for about one hundred and fifty. The tables and tea equippages were contributed by the ladies who presided at the tea-tables; everything else was supplied to the order of Squire Brown. And what a gathering was there! What a collection of bright, jolly faces, browned by the weather, glowing with health, and beaming with smiles that came straight from the light and happy hearts. From Greyabbey, Carrowdore, Cardy, Ballyboley, Ballywalter, and a score of other places, the sons and daughters of the sod mustered in strong force for a night of harmless amusement. At this remote period it would be impossible to enumerate all who took part in the memorable proceedings now to be related, but the description would be sadly incomplete were no mention made of such as can be remembered. Amongst the daughters of the Sod there were in the old barn that night Mary Ann M'Cullough, of Dorrey's Hill; Miss Johnston, of Ballydoonan; Miss M'Clattery, Miss Mawhinney and Miss Jane Mawhinney, the Misses Jenny and Sally Corry, and Miss Mary M'Kay, of Dunover; the Kerrs, of Islandtim; Miss Mary Murphy, Miss Matty Brown and Miss Eliza Brown, Miss Matty M'Givern, Miss Annie Moorehead; Miss Susan Mathers, Miss Maria Murphy (a lady who was always "bad wi' a cauld,"), Miss Nelly Davidson, Miss Ann Jane Wilson, Miss Mary Muckatee, Miss Katy M'Cormick, and Miss Jane Mawhinney, all of Cardy;

DORREY'S HILL

from Ballyboley there were Miss Whuff, Miss Jane Armstrong, the Misses Rachel, Esther and Jean Moore, Miss Mary and Miss Eliza Askin, Miss Jane and Miss Eliza M'Kay, Miss Betty Beck, Miss Molly Beck, Mary Fisher, Kate Kearney, Nancy Kearney, Betty Bowden, and Bell M'Cance. The Sons of the Son included all our acquaintances, now familiar to the reader, and their names do not require recapitulation. John Cleland, of Cardy; William and Robert Byers, Sam M'Kee and James M'Kee, Hugh Ferguson, William John Davidson, of Ballygraingey, and others wore rosettes as members of committee.

By and by there was a bustling about the door, and the word passed round—

"Here they're comin', an' the Squire's wi' them."

Just then Harry O'Neill entered, his blushing wife leaning upon his arm and glancing timidly round. They were closely followed by Johnnie Hunter, and his fair Jeannie, while the Squire himself brought up the rere. This was more than people had expected from a man of Squire Brown's habits, and they were not slow to appreciate the compliment. Every man rose to his feet, and the cheer which burst forth was such as had never before greeted the ears of Squire Brown.

At one end of the room a platform had been constructed by David Morrow, of Ballyboley, and a table was here laid for "the quality." The Squire and his friends were conducted hither by Dominie Harvey, and the tea-table was presided over by Mrs. Byers, of Ballyboley House, a lady who was very popular in the neighbourhood.

The ringing of a large bell was the signal for commencing proceedings, and the silence which had for several minutes prevailed was instantly succeeded by the deafening clatter of spoons and tea cups and the incessant hum of conversation.

Outside of the buildings, suspended over huge turf fires, were several large boilers, borrowed from the congregations of

Carrowdore, Balbriggan, Ballyblack, and Greyabbey. Tea was not so freely consumed in those days as it is now, but there was a profusion of it on this occasion. The committee had ordered two dozen large crocks, and into these the tea was poured from the boilers. Into these crocks the stewards dipped large tin measures, each of which held at least a quart, from which they filled their kettles.

The rush to and fro was terrific. Every steward seemed determined that the tea-maker upon whom he was to wait should have the first kettle of tea and the first tray laden with currant loaf, cut into huge slices of fully two inches in thickness. The gathering was, in fact, up to a certain point, simply a country "suree," and such, being familiar to most of our readers, requires but little description. Stewards jostled each other as they struggled to reach their respective tables, holding aloft large trays laden with piles of bread, puffing and perspiring as they did so, and "jawing" one another freely. A casual note-taker, who for amusement, might have jotted down the phrases as they reached his ear, would likely have presented a report somewhat as follows:—

"Min' whaur yer pittin' yer feet, boy!"

"A wuz niver axed yit if A had a mooth on me!"

"Whaur's Sam M'Givern?"

"Sam, A wush ye wud quate glowerin' aboot ye, an' bring me anither kettle o' tay!"

"Teer me up, Mary Ann, but ye micht as weel empty it in a dyke sheugh as doon them fowks' throats!"

"Wully Harper, is the breid din? There wasnae half enough for my table; no yin got mair than half a dozen slices!"

"Cum here wi' them Sally Lunns,* boy! Clod them doon here!"

---

* The Bath delicacy 'Sally Lunn Bun' is part bun, part bread and part cake.

DORREY'S HILL

"Davy Morrow, fetch me a pickle shugor oot o' that crock unner the table!"

And Davey dives under the table to find a local celebrity known as "Shugor Pokits" with his mouth full of the sugar, and stuffing handfuls of it into his pockets.

The noise is chiefly caused by the attendants and tea-makers. Most of the eaters are attending to their business in a business-like manner, and the provisions disappear with magic-like rapidity. By and by the jaws move less freely; cups are sent in with a "Nae mair, thank ye, mem;" pockets are slyly stretched to their utmost capacity! The sugar bowl and cream jug are passed round, and "clodding" begins in real earnest.

For another chapter must be reserved a description of the Punch Ball which followed, with account of some lively incidents which occurred thereat including the "Royal Quadrille" by local celebrities and Dominie Harvey's famous County Down song, written for the occasion.

CHAPTER XXXIX

ANOTHER PUNCH BALL

IT was not long until the tea tables were carried out of doors, and piled in an adjoining field. An address of welcome and congratulation had previously been drawn up to the Squire and his friends, and this was read by Taylor, the schoolmaster, amid great enthusiasm. The Squire made a suitable reply, and left shortly afterwards, accompanied by his daughter and son-in-law. Johnnie Hunter and his fair Jeannie remained till the close of the proceedings.

No sooner had the squire left than Davey Hamilton, who had been appointed Master of Ceremonies, set about having arrangements made for the dance. The rasping and scraping of Hughey Finlay's fiddle, as that celebrity tuned his instrument, set every tongue a-wagging; and there was a hearty cheer, accompanied by clapping of hands, as Mr. Hugh Fergus, stepping nimbly across the room, with arms akimbo, bowed gracefully to Miss Marget Cameron, and secured the companionship of that lady for the first quadrille. Leading his blushing partner to the head of the room, he was quickly followed by William John Doherty, of Greyabbey, who led by the hand Miss Betty Gibson; then came Miss Mary Woods, leaning on the arm of Teugh M'Kay, and Hannah Lynn, supported by John Bailey, who, as he crushed through the crowd, was continually murmuring in his partner's ear—"Oh, Hannah Lynn, you're the girl I love."

Just when the parties were in readiness for what Davie Hamilton styled the "Royal Quadrille," and Hughey Finlay had made a grand preliminary flourish of his bow, a string of his fiddle snapped with a sharp report.

"Deil tak' yer fiddle!" growled M'Kay, as he slyly squeezed Mary's waist.

"How provoking, my dear," whispered Mr. Fergus to Marget.

"He ocht tae keep better catgut," remarked Marget, in response.

"Dear me! such a vulgar name for a violin string," said Fergus, "I wonder another term is not employed."

"Ye shud pit it in French," laughed Marget, "or else be like yin o' the M'Kee lasses."

"What was that, my dear?"

"Oh, she went intil a music shop in Belfast yin day for fiddle strings, an' sez she till the man—'If ye pleese, sur, wud ye give sixpence worth o' pooshey's' bowels.'"

Marget's partner seemed quite shocked at this specimen of over-strained politeness, and he appeared to feel relieved when all was in readiness for the dance.

"Aff ye gang!" shouted Davey Hamilton, and off they went, slowly at first, but warming to their work as they proceeded, and reminding us forcibly of some lines recently contributed by friend Corrigan, of Dublin:

> At first they moved slowly, with caution and grace,
> Like horses when just setting out on a race;
> For dancers at balls, like horses at races,
> Must amble a little to show off their paces.
> Now draperies whirl, now petticoats fly,
> And ankles, at least, are exposed to the eye;
> And they still bear in mind, as they're turning each other,
> The proverb—"one good turn's deserving another."

Everything must have an end, and so had the Royal Quadrille. Signs of fatigue were visible in the faces of the ladies, and the merry spin was brought to a termination by Hugh

Fergus throwing his arms round his partner and saluting her with a smacking kiss. Wm. John Doherty, Hugh M'Kay, and John Bailey followed the example so worthily set them, and the quadrille party retired to their seats amid loud applause.

This was but the prelude to the real fun. There was a rush to the floor for a "Country Dance," after the good old fashion, and many a rosy-cheeked, bouncing lass beat the floor that night with flying feet, some of them being heard to boast that they "wur jest twenty-seven inches roon the waist."

"Come, Hughey!" shouted Sam M'Givern, to the fiddler, "mak' her bum! Gie us a screed o' Nora Crena!" and at it they went. The onlookers paid considerable attention to the selection of partners by the Sons of the Sod, and those who were present still recollect that the following couples were almost inseparable during the night:—Bell M'Cance and Alick Riggs; Mary Murphy and Bab Lowry; Jeanny Mawhinney and Alick Watson; Katy Muckatee and Hugh Fergus; Miss M'Clatterty and Davey Morrow; Miss Whuff and John Lowry; Annie Moorhead and John Reid; Nancy Kearney and Jamey Fisher; Bell M'Cartney and William M'Cay; Sarah Corry and Wully Wilson; Eliza Johnston and John Cleland; Rebecca Cowan and Frank Wright; Eliza Shanks and Sammy Reid; Bell Herron and Hugh M'Kay.

Songs and recitations varied the entertainment. A local singing master, named M'Kinley, was present, and he was always ready and willing to oblige the company. He was not a handsome man by any means, and he possessed a remarkably long and pointed nose. Mr. David Stormont, of Newtownards, speaking of meeting M'Kinley once, said—"First I saw a nose coming round the corner, and then I saw M'Kinley." A good story is told in connection with a singing class taught by him in Ballyvester Schoolhouse. On quarterly nights he insisted upon every male pupil composing a verse of poetry and singing

ANOTHER PUNCH BALL

it. At that time Johnnie Gordon, of Ballyhay, was a stirring youth, and he bore the singing master no good will. When it came Johnnie's turn he rattled out the following verse, his voice being almost drowned towards the conclusion by shouts of laughter:—

> "When the deil he entered swine,
>   The herd for to destroy;
> Yin lang nosed boar he left behin'—
>   M'Kinley, you're the boy!"

M'Kinley sang several songs in the barn that night, which to this day are well known in the neighbourhood, notable amongst them being the one commencing:—

> "Hannah Lynn she has got wed;
>   Fifty poun' and a feather bed;
> Hangers neat an' blankets clean,
>   A bonnie wee lass, but 'squinkin' een.'"

Then followed Jamey Fisher with his "quilting" song, the first verse of which ran thus:—

> "Oh, the first of March I'll never forget,
>   A quiltin' in M'Murray's met,
> Ribbons an' laces sae braw an' sae gran',
> But what dae ye think, they kiss'd the rag man,
>   Down, down, down, derry down!"

The palm, however, so far as singing was concerned, fell to our old friend, Dominie Harvey. The good old man composed a special song for the occasion. It ran as follows:—

SONS OF THE SOD

Kind ladies and good gentlemen, come listen to my song,
It's of yourselves I mean to sing, so pray don't think it long,
For sure the world nowhere contains such people of renown
As the girls and boys that I could name, all in Sweet County Down.

Now, first to give the preference, where preference is due,
There's a lady here to-night just sitting full in view,
Her name this night it is O'Neill, although it once was Brown,
And she's the fairest of her sex throughout old County Down.

And next there's bonnie Jeannie, who comes from off the hill,
Young Johnnie Hunter married her, and not against her will;
Oh, may God bless these two young wives, and never on them frown,
And may they every year increase the stock of County Down!

Long live the Ballyboley boys, and flourish evermore;
And long live Wullie Yeaman, the Mayor of Carrowdore,
Who rubs his mare with wisps of notes when he's for Newton boun'
No richer man lives anywhere in all broad County Down.

There's the "Ballyboley Hoogher," M'Briar is his name,
And honest Sam M'Givern my notice too must claim;
There's Teugh M'Kay, and Morrow, too, who lives near Greyab town,
No man can better coffins make in all sweet County Down.

And then there's Hughey Hamilton—a boy so fond of cheese—
John Gibson who can stories tell that's always sure to please;
There's handsome Whulty Regan, too, that tailor of renown,
Who's fit to put his tapeline round the best in County Down.

ANOTHER PUNCH BALL

But if I spoke about them all, I'd keep you here too long,
There's just one girl I wish to name before I close my song,
The sweetest, dearest, brightest girl that ever wore a gown,
A marquis she could captivate, this maid of County Down.

Oh, dearly do I love this lass of Ballyboley Moss,
To guess the letters of her name you won't be at a loss;
If that dear girl won't marry me, myself I'll shoot or drown,
For she is all the world to me, this Queen of County Down.

Now, fill your glasses to the brim and drink with me a toast—
"The ladies!" bless their loving hearts, they are our pride and boast:
Long live the O'Neills and Hunters, too, may joy their marriage crown,
Success attend the boys and girls of dear old County Down!

Cheer upon cheer followed every verse of the Dominie's song, and the old gentleman was so delighted with the applause that he quite forgot how many glasses of punch he was quaffing. An hour afterwards he was peacefully sleeping in a corner of the barn, with somebody's overcoat spread upon him and a big currant loaf under his head for a pillow.

But little more remains to be told. Harry O'Neill took up his abode at the Big House. The Squire appointed Johnnie Hunter as his agent in the room of Ben the bailiff who was buried at midnight where four roads joined, and a stake driven through his breast, as was the custom with suicides. Harry O'Neill paid the rent of Widow Hunter's farm while she lived, but that was not many years. The dear old lady never recovered from the shock caused by her son's arrest, and her health gradually failed. She now sleeps in the quiet graveyard at Greyabbey. Light lie the sod on her worthy breast!

Squire Brown died, leaving all that he possessed to his daughter. Harry, anxious to change his quiet mode of life, induced his wife to sell the property, and the two, accompanied by their little ones, sailed for New York. Johnnie Hunter, unable to bear the separation, soon realised what effects he had, and with his wife and little son crossed the broad Atlantic also, to seek a home in that generous country which has so often stretched out its inviting hands to old Ireland and to its warm-hearted, but oft-times misrepresented

SONS OF THE SOD.

GLOSSARY

A

a	I have
a'	all
aback	at the back of
aboon	above
aboot	about
acause	because
ae	one
aff	off
affen	often
afore	before
agen	again, against
aheid	ahead
ahint	behind
ain	own
akwelly	actually
alang	along
aloo	allow
amang	among
an'	and
ance	once
anither	another
apen	open
a'thegither	altogether
athoot	without
atween	between

auld	old
ava	at all
awa'	away
aye	always
baith	both
bakit	baked
bannocks	round, flattish cakes of (usually) oatmeal
bate	beat, beaten
begood	began
behauden	beholden
ben	inside
bigg	build
birl	spin
biz	be
blaws	blows
bleezes	blazes
blether (n)	one who talks nonsense
blethers	nonsense
bluid	blood
bocht	bought
body	person
bowster	bolster
brave	fine
bravely	well
braw	fine
breid	bread
brocht	brought
buddy	person

GLOSSARY

ca'	call
cannae	can't
carlie	old man
caul	cold
cauld	cold
caupie	wooden bowl or cup
chittyrans	wrens
chockit	choked
claes	clothes
clappit	clapped
clod	throw
clodding	eating and drinking
coast	cost
coortin'	courting
coupt	turned over
couthie	sociable
crack	chat
crackin'	chatting
crater	creature
crayter	creature
creeshed	greased
crouse	proud
cud	could
cudnae	couldn't
cummed	came
dae	do
dain	doing
daith	death
danner	walk, wander

dannered	walked
daur	dare
daur	door
daurnae	daren't
dee	die
deid	dead
deil	devil
denner	dinner
didnae	didn't
din	done
dinna	don't
dint	don't
disturbit	disturbed
diz	does
diznae	doesn't
dochtor	daughter
dokter	doctor
dooble	double
doon	down
doot	doubt
drappie	drop (of alcohol)
dree	endure, bear, suffer
dug	dog
dunch	nudge
duskis	dusky
e'e	eye
e'en	eyes
een	eyes
efter	after

GLOSSARY

eneuch	enough
enuch	enough
et	ate, eaten
ether	either
farder	farther
farls	flat cakes of bread
fecht	fight
fechtin'	fighting
feered	afraid
fin'	find
flair	floor
flee	fly
fleechin'	coaxing, begging
fleed	flew
fleers	grins, grimaces
flooer	flour, flower
forbye	besides
Forgeyson	Ferguson
forrit	forward
fowk	folk
frae	from
freen	friend
frichtened	frightened
friens	friends
fu'	full
fule	fool
fun'	found
fur	for
fut	foot

gang	go
gars	makes, forces
gaun	going
gie	give
gie an'	very
gied	gave
giss	goose
gizen	be parched
glowerin'	looking, staring
gra	liking
grun	ground
gruppit	grabbed, gripped
Guid	God
guid	good
hadnae	hadn't
hae	have
haen	had
haesnae	hasn't
haggard	stackyard
hale	whole
hame	home
haud	hold
hauf	half
heech	high
heecht	height
heelan	highland
heerd	heard
heerin'	hearing

GLOSSARY

heicht	height
heid	head
herm	harm
heth	faith
hoise	hoist
hoo	how
hooer	hour
hoonaniver	however
hoor	hour
hoose	house
hoots	fie
hunner	hundred
imperent	impudent
intil	into
ir	are
ither	other
ivery	every
jest	just
jookin'	ducking and diving, moving in a surreptitious way
jookit	ducked
keekit	peeked
ken	know
kent	knew
keruyus	curious
kilt	killed
kin'	kind

knockit	knocked
knowes	hillocks
kye	cows
laft	loft
lan'	land
lang	long
langer	longer
lauch	laugh
lauchin'	laughing
lave	leave
lea	leave
lee	leave
lee	lie
leeshins	lessons
leev	leave
leev	live
leeve	live
leevin'	living
lichtit	lit
liftit	lifted
likit	liked
lisens	licence
loanin'	lane
lowe	flame
luckit	looked
lug	ear
lukit	looked
lum	fireplace

GLOSSARY

mair	more
maist	most
maun	must
meat	food
meent	meant
meer	mare
meet	meat
merches	borders
mester	master
micht	might
michtnae	mightn't
mither	mother
mony	many
mooth	mouth
muckle	much
Muckleboy	McIlboy
nae	no
naethin'	nothing
nane	none
nether	neither
nicht	night
nippit	nipped
niver	never
nixt	next
no'	not
noggin	wooden eating or drinking vessel
noo	now
nor	than
notis	notice

o'	of
ocht	anything
ocht	ought
ony	any
onywae	anyway
oorsels	ourselves
oot	out
ordinar	usual
ower	over
pad	path
parritch	porridge
pawky	sly, cunning
peeces	pieces
pert	part
pickle	small amount
piggin	wooden vessel with a handle for carrying or ladling milk
pit	put
plantin	plantation of trees
pleesintest	pleasantest
plewin	ploughing
pooshey	pussy
pow	head
pressie	cupboard
pu'	pull
puir	poor
puzhin	poison
pye	pay

GLOSSARY

quate	quiet
quer	strangely
residenter	inhabitant
rether	rather
richt	right
rid	red
riz	rose
roon	round
sabbin	sobbing
sae	so
saft	soft
sair	sore
sare	sore
sate	seat
saut	salt
sayries	serious
saze	seize
scaur	scare
screed	rasp
seeck	sick
shair	sure
shaps	shops
sherper	sharper
sheugh	ditch
shooder	shoulder
shoon	shoes
shudnae	shouldn't

shugh	ditch
shughlin	shuffling, shambling
shugor	sugar
sich	such
sicht	sight
siller	silver
skolard	scholar
skule	school
skunnered	disgusted, fed up with
slackit	slacked, eased
slippit	slipped
soart	sort
soo	sow
soon	sound
spauk	spoke, spoken
speerin'	asking, requesting
speir	enquire
squinkin	squinting
stae	stay
stanes	stones
stap	stop
stappage	stammer
stappit	stopped
streecht	stretched
strek	strike
stroops	spouts
sughin'	blowing
suin	soon
suree	soiree
sut	sat

GLOSSARY

syne	thereupon, next
tae	to
ta'en	taken
taen	taken
tak	take
talkit	talked
Tamson	Thomson, Thompson
tangs	tongs
tay	tea
teer	tear
tell't	told
the day	today
thegither	together
thocht	thought
thon	that, those
thonner	yonder
thoosan	thousand
thrawin'	awkward, stubborn
till	to
tither	other
tuk	took
twa	two
twal	twelve
twunty	twenty
unner	under
velye	value

wa'	wall
waddin'	wedding
wae	way
waens	children
waur	worse
wean	child
weazen	windpipe
wecht	weight
weeda	widow
weel	well
weshes	washes
weskit	waistcoat
wha	who
whauraboots	whereabouts
whaur	where
wheen	number
whins	whin bushes, gorse
whun	when
whun	whin, furze, gorse
whuppit	whipped
whussel	whistle
wi'	with
wipit	wiped
wrang	wrong
wrasle	wrestle
wudnae	wouldn't
wull	will
wundey	window
wunnae	won't
wur	were

GLOSSARY

wurl	world
wurnae	weren't
wush	wish
wuts	wits
wuznae	wasn't
ye	you
yer	your, you're
yin	one
yince	once
yit	yet

Printed in Great
Britain
by Amazon